'*From Zero to CEO* is an excellent book that does a lot more than just show you how to build a thriving business from home. It takes you on an inspiring journey, told by someone who has come from humble beginnings yet achieved success. So, if you want the fast-track to create a business from home, read this book.'

Dale Beaumont, Founder and CEO of Business Blueprint

'When you are looking for a true understanding of the entrepreneurial journey of building a highly successful home-based business from nothing, you cannot go past reading *From Zero to CEO*. This is a truly inspirational and motivational book written by someone who came from having the world seemingly stacked against her to rise far above the clouds of success.'

Peter J White AM, MAICD, Managing Director of the FBAA, Chairman of the Global Board of Governors, IMBF

'I wish to congratulate Victoria Coster, CEO of Credit Fix Solutions, on her book about starting and running a small business *From Zero to CEO*. The book details everything a start-up business owner needs to know. It can also serve as a refresher for those businesses that are already operating. The book is invaluable as today a start-up business owner needs more than just luck to operate a business. Years ago, a small business owner could start up a business with a few dollars and make a success.

'Today, running a small business requires a more sophisticated approach. Due to Australia being a global village, business owners face competition from overseas and locally. Due to the myriad regulations and compliance issues, a small business owner needs to be aware of the pitfalls and ensure they build firm foundations from the outset.

'This book will help you understand the maze and create an awareness of what you need to do to avoid failure and make yourself stand out from the crowd.

'I recommend this book and will be pleased to promote this through our vast network to assist every small business owner. Again, congratulations!'

Anne Nalder, Founder and CEO, Small Business Association of Australia

FROM ZERO TO CEO

VICTORIA COSTER

© Victoria Coster 2020

The moral rights of the author have been asserted.

A catalogue record for this book is available from the National Library of Australia

ISBN: 978-0-6487963-8-1

All rights reserved. Except as permitted under *The Australian Copyright Act 1968* (for example, a fair dealing for the purposes of study, research, criticism or review), no part of this book may be reproduced, stored in a retrieval system, communicated or transmitted in any form or by any means without prior written permission. All inquiries should be made to the author.

Cover design by Tess McCabe
Internal design by Production Works
Printed in Australia by SOS Print + Media

10 9 8 7 6 5 4 3 2 1

Disclaimer: The material in this publication is in the nature of general comment only, and neither purports nor intends to be advice. Readers should not act on the basis of any matter in this publication without considering (and if appropriate taking) professional advice with due regard to their own particular circumstances. The author expressly disclaims all and any liability to any person, whether a purchaser of this publication or not, in respect of anything and the consequences of anything done or omitted to be done by any such person in reliance, whether whole or partial, upon the whole or any part of the contents of this publication.

CONTENTS

Dedication **vii**

Introduction **1**

Chapter 1   Getting *you* right first! **5**

Chapter 2   Getting started **21**

Chapter 3   Finding your target customers **39**

Chapter 4   Managing your systems **47**

Chapter 5   A step-by-step guide to social media **59**

Chapter 6   Getting visible **73**

Chapter 7   Network and connect **89**

Chapter 8   The super-dry but necessary **99**

Chapter 9   Customer service **111**

DEDICATION

I dedicate this book to the following people, without whom it would not have been possible.

My amazing husband, Jardine, who has been so patient with me and always believed I can achieve more than I think I can. To my mentors and friends, Darrell Weekes, Peter White, Hank de Jonge, Rick Jones and Dale Beaumont, who have all believed in me and encouraged me to be all that I can be as a business owner as well as helped me to get to where I am today. To my family and my friends, who have seen me struggle, seen me at my lowest; thank you for never giving up on me even when I was completely lost!

Thank you, Father, thank you Jesus, thank you Holy Spirit, thank you Mother Mary, thank you all the saints and angels in Heaven.

For all the blessings in my life, for my beautiful family; my husband, my rock, my heart, my best friend; for our children; for my wonderful friends; for my business and my achievements.

For the endless joy in my heart, and the peace that I have in my soul, that my journey on this earth has not been wasted, that I have loved, I have been loved, I have dreamed and that I have seen my dreams come true.

In Jesus' name I pray for all of you, that you can experience the kind of peace and joy that I have found in my life, and I pray for peace and success for you.

INTRODUCTION

Starting a business is no easy feat. According to the Australian Bureau of Statistics, more than 60 per cent of small businesses stop their operation within the first three years of their start-up journey. You may think that is because of money but, in a lot of cases, it's because the business owner lacks skills or lacks a real *'why'* they started the business.

We're not educated at school on how to start a business, and business courses at university are mainly theoretical, so you still have to go and get experience in the workplace to learn the real thing.

Then, there's the cost of setting up a business, learning the skills you need, and having the confidence in yourself to give it a go.

Business courses can be expensive and are mostly aimed at business owners who want to grow and who have already been trading for some time. There are some cheaper college courses that you can do, but they are split into topics, and therefore you could spend years studying different aspects of business before you can put all the pieces of the puzzle together. Motivational courses are great at helping you feel good about yourself, but they don't give you the actual tools you need to run a business.

Business mentors are amazing. I have a few mentors around me and I wouldn't be where I am today without their help and support. But they cost money. A mentor may be out of your reach at the start of your journey, so consider this book your mentoring guide for the first few months until you start earning money, then you can look at getting mentors or business coaches involved.

When I started my business I had nothing. I was a single mum in a housing unit. I made many mistakes, jumped into a new business with no business skills and waded through my first 12 months not really knowing what I was doing from day to day or week to week.

I've put this book together to encourage and help people who may have a great small business idea to confidently start a small business that they can run from home, with pretty much no money (except the $29.95 for this book and some minor costs for printing business cards and other small marketing expenses). In this easy-to-follow, step-by-step guide, I've combined motivational training and guidance on all areas of business that you need to get started. I've put all the pieces of the puzzle together for you!

The idea for this book came to me a few years ago when I was having coffee with another mum at my sons' primary school. Before she got married, she was a highly skilled, successful interior designer, but she was going through a terrible divorce and had not been in the workforce for 10 years. She had a great idea of putting hampers together and selling them locally or online. However, she was too scared to start and did not know where to begin. I tried to encourage her but, really, what she needed was a practical book on how to start, which was easy to follow. There was nothing out there to help her, though.

It frustrated me back then, and still does today, that there are no holistic guides to starting a home business. You need to spend thousands of dollars on higher education *or* make a lot of mistakes *or* spend years doing courses before you can put it all together.

So, I've put all my learnings and skills together and created this book, which will help anyone start a business from home, if they follow it chapter by chapter. Although the book is short, it's hands-on. I'll encourage you to stop at stages throughout the book and action what I've taught you. By the end of it, you should be running a successful small business from home.

I have kept it simple. This is not meant as a guide to running a large business or earning millions of dollars – although it does give you the bones to create a structure that could! It's meant for those of you who maybe have young kids to look after, or have been through a life event that means you need to work from home or, for whatever reason, you just want to start and run your own micro business from home to give you the time and flexibility to live a happy life!

From Zero to CEO could also help those of you who have already started a business but need some guidance in some areas.

I hope that this book not only gives you a means to an end but also allows you to create something beautiful, something you can be proud of.

If I can just help one person out there to start a small business from home, then the months of work I've put into this book are totally worth it.

I'd love to hear your feedback, as I'm happy to help you along the way. My details are given at the end of the book so you can reach out if the need arises.

CHAPTER 1
GETTING *YOU* RIGHT FIRST!

- **LOVE**
- **HEALTH**
- **HAPPINESS**

THERE'S NO POINT even thinking about starting a business until you've got *you* right first.

Without a healthy and positive mindset, you won't get far. This is the first and most important chapter of this book, and it is an absolute 'must do' for you to be successful in whatever business you are looking to start.

I wouldn't be where I am today, a successful CEO of a national company, without first having worked on myself as a person.

Now, please get a notepad and jot down notes as you go through the book. You will be able to refer to these notes when you put together your action plan for your business start-up. Writing things down helps you commit information to memory, and your notepad will in fact also become your very first draft business plan of sorts once you've actioned all the chapters!

It's important you understand why I've written this book.

My life started in a government-funded home, in a town called Stevenage – around an hour's drive north of London in the UK. My family was far from rich. I promised myself, as a child, that when I grew up, I would do everything possible to *not* be poor. To be honest, I'm grateful for all my experiences, even the bad ones, because without them I wouldn't be who I am, or where I am financially, today.

My family immigrated to Australia when I was 16 in 1996. I started my business in 2014 and, at the time, I was living in commission housing, in a small two-bedroom unit in West Sydney with my son, Nikolai. I had been through a horrendous divorce, which had left me mentally scarred. I was in my early thirties, earning a meagre wage working long hours for somebody else's business, and I hardly had time to spend with my son.

I quit my job one day out of frustration and spent around three months focusing on spending time with my son and working on my mental and spiritual health.

You may have been through tough times too, or maybe you are going through them now, so it's vital that you work on yourself first. You need to be tough enough to start your business, and then run it successfully too.

> 'Everything can be taken from a man but one thing: the last of the human freedoms – to choose one's attitude in any given set of circumstances, to choose one's own way.'
>
> —VIKTOR FRANKL

I'm a true believer that giving back is one of the most important things we can do with our time. Therefore, I've written down everything I've learnt since starting my business in 2014, and I've created this book to help those who want to start a business but simply don't know where to begin. I want to help others to achieve their dreams too. When I started in business, there wasn't a book like this around, and I stumbled my way through for a long time. I'm hoping that this book will help others like me to get their business started without so much stumbling!

TAKE A GOOD LOOK AT YOURSELF

First, let's look at where you are on a personal and mental level so we can get you on the right track to be able to start a new business. Have you been through tough times like I had, or maybe you are currently struggling with life? You can't feed your history and feed your destiny at the same time. Feed what's right, don't feed self-pity. You must let go of what didn't work, or what has hurt you. Put your energy into believing in new beginnings, in great things from God. Don't feed the fear, don't feed the offence.

Ask yourself, 'Am I going to keep watering these weeds, or am I going to water the flowers?'

Sometimes God ends things that we don't understand. He closes the door. So, look forward to the new and amazing things ahead! You will come into a new season of joy and blessings.

Let this chapter be the first chapter of a beautiful new journey for you!

The most important questions you need to ask yourself right now are, 'Why am I doing this? Why do I want to start my own business?' Do you want more time at home with your children? Do you want more time to start hobbies, or to travel? Would you like to get more involved with charity work?

Write down your *'why'* on a Post-it Note and stick it somewhere you can read it every day.

When you have your *'why'*, start putting up your vision board. I just printed out pictures on a $70 printer and stuck them on the wall above my desk with Blu Tack. There's no need to get too fancy at this point!

Do you have a vision board? If you do, have a look at it. Look at it every day. Do you have some mantras up there? One of my favourites is:

> 'My heart is at ease knowing that what was meant for me will never miss me, and that what misses me was never meant for me.'
>
> —IMAM AL-SHAFI'I, 8TH CENTURY MUSLIM JURIST

WHAT'S YOUR DAILY ROUTINE?

Now you've got your vision board up, let's get onto the next thing, which is getting yourself into a good routine, starting with when you first wake up.

We are all the sum of our choices and actions. Today is just an echo of yesterday, and tomorrow will bring what we brought today. So, live each day to your very best. If you stumble, it's OK! Just get back up and keep going. There is no right or wrong or good and bad, there are simply your choices. Choose wisely and be gentle.

> 'Do not worry about tomorrow, for tomorrow will worry about itself.'
>
> —MATTHEW 6:34 (NIV)

It's not that successful people are necessarily smarter than everyone else. It's more likely that they simply make better choices and *act*. Life will either make you or break you. At the end of the day, it's your choices that define your direction, not your IQ.

How do you start your day?

I start mine by thanking the Lord for another day. Then I slowly mentally list a few things that I am grateful for (usually while sipping a strong black coffee, of course – I'm only human, and a mum, and a wife, and a CEO, after all). Some mornings I'm just grateful that I can get out of bed pain-free and for five minutes of peace and quiet to read some mindful sayings or enjoy the garden before the day gets hectic.

Try to think of three things you are grateful for, as soon as you wake up, and you will start to notice that your days go more peacefully. You will feel more positive, and this will have a flow-on effect for the rest of the day.

We aren't separate from everyone else. When we suffer, everyone suffers. If you take care of your mind, you take care of the world.

> 'Sometimes people let the same problem make them miserable for years when they could just say, "So what." That's one of my favorite things to say.'
>
> —ANDY WARHOL

I find if I make sure that I keep the following three daily activities in my routine, I can get out of bed with a positive mindset and retain that mindset the entire day:

1. **Being grateful when I wake up.** Whether this is to God, Jesus, or just put out to the universe, being grateful makes you realise how much you have to be thankful for in your life.
2. **Daily exercise.** You'll find that even a short walk, with a little sunshine, will improve your mood.

3. **Ensuring you have some *me* time** Shut the phone off at 5pm, or earlier if you can, and spend time meditating or in prayer. Make time for family and friends, too.

I know so many people who work late hours, and sometimes I know that we must. I have had some days that seemed to never end. But most days I shut off from business mode at around 4pm to make time for my family and for myself. In my opinion, being successful isn't bragging that you are busy, that you've just done another 16-hour day. I think success is when you can manage to finish your work within a few hours every day and then the rest of the day is yours to do with as you please.

> 'Do not despise your own place and hour. Every place is under the stars, every place is the center of the world.'
>
> —JOHN BURROUGHS

LOVE YOURSELF

If I could go back and say something to my 20-year-old self, it would be 'Go with your gut.' So many times, in my twenties, I listened too much to others and to media. I read magazines that told me I had to look a certain way and, if I didn't, I wasn't good enough. Media and society told me I needed money and a flash car to be happy. If only I had listened to my inner voice a bit more, I wouldn't have made half the decisions I did.

I married someone because he threw money and expensive gifts at me, and then he emotionally abused me, saying I was never good enough for him, that he had made me all that I was, and he had wasted his money and time on me. I stayed in that relationship way too long and came out emotionally scarred. I'm proud that I escaped when I did. When my son was nearly two years old, I managed to escape with a suitcase and nowhere to live. Luckily, I had family to help me out. I know many others who weren't as lucky as I was.

I've raised my son with no child support and at one point I was living on friends' couches!

For all you single ladies out there, don't marry someone because of money or success. Often these sorts of people don't really have money anyway, it's all borrowed. Take your time when making the decision to spend your life with someone. Look for real qualities like honesty, humility and kindness. And, for the lovely men out there who have been through horrific times, please do the same. I encourage you to speak up if you need help too.

Stop reading magazines that tell you to look skinny or ripped. Turn off the TV channels that tell you that you need to look 21! Look at yourself in the mirror and tell yourself you are beautiful or handsome. You are amazing. Every day, wake up and be the best version of you that you can be. You can only ever compete with yourself. Just keep on trying to be a little better than you were the day before.

Don't look at others and compare yourself to them. Look at yourself. Are you underachieving? Are you happy? What can you do to improve your day, your life, your dreams?

Don't be envious of someone who has something you want. Go and do the hard work they have done to get themselves there and then you will be shaking their hand! Don't waste years of your life having to recover from toxic relationships that you can easily avoid. If you've already made that mistake, start anew today. Make the choice to love yourself and change your mindset.

I love to remember the following quote when I'm having a stressful day with clients:

> 'The people I deal with today will be meddling, ungrateful, arrogant, dishonest, jealous and surly. They are like this because they can't tell good from evil. But I have seen the beauty of good, and the ugliness of evil, and have recognised that the wrongdoer has a nature related to my own – not of the same blood or birth, but the same mind, and possessing a share of the divine. And so, none of them can hurt me.'
>
> —MARCUS AURELIUS, DIED 180 AD

TAKE CARE OF YOUR HEALTH

For me, personally, my mental health and my spiritual health are equally as important as my physical health. If I am not mentally and spiritually OK, then I will not have a good day at all. It's hard to juggle children, work, staff and personal relationships on the best of days. Faith is also the key to my inner peace. I found God and Jesus in a beautiful little church, St Bernadette's, in Dundas Valley, New South Wales, attached to my son's Catholic primary school. Up until that point I thought there was no meaning to life, to all that we do. I thought that we simply struggled through, pasted on a smile and that was that.

I could not have been further from the truth. Jesus loves us so much. He is the Son of God. He will come back to judge the world. And you can't tell me any different! I'm not going to preach, but I may drop a verse in here or there, for positive motivation. May I suggest, if you're curious, you go and get a Bible, and just read the New Testament, starting with Matthew. As you go along your journey, enjoy your imperfect, beautiful self. Be patient with your spiritual growth. It can be slow, but don't give up. Surround yourself with love and good people, and this will all come back to you ten-fold.

I'm telling you, my soul overflows with joy and love and happiness because I found Him. In Jesus' name, I have walked away from all the pain in my life. I am whole and I am loved, and I am never alone. It doesn't matter if everything around me goes wrong because my faith makes me stronger than any crap the universe can throw at me.

Having a good heart and having honest and humble intentions in business are important if you want to have a long-term successful business. You will never be successful if you have the wrong intentions in offering a service or product to others. People will see through you. They will recognise that you don't come from a place of love and honesty, and they won't sign on the dotted line.

Yes, of course business is about profit. We will get to that later. But I truly believe that if you don't have honest intentions to help people with whatever service you are offering, you will not achieve your dreams of success in business. So, getting *you* right first is key to making your business dream a reality. *Character is everything!*

KEEPING A POSITIVE MINDSET

A great way to get into a positive mindset is to ask yourself, 'What are my miracles?'

Some days can be tough. The children are playing up, there are six loads of washing to be done (I recently remarried and inherited three stepchildren – and let me tell you, going from a single mum with one child for 10 years to being married and becoming the Brady Bunch gave me at least another 20 grey hairs). Oh, and then there are difficult clients, problems to fix for staff, and a bottle of wine staring at me in the kitchen saying, 'Drink me, drink me.' Again, I'll reiterate my previous quote about not worrying about tomorrow.

So, what are your miracles?

One of my miracles was my son. Another was being approved for housing after my divorce. Some miracles might be small – 'Life is in the details' I heard someone say once. Sometimes just taking a deep breath and thinking about some small precious moments in your life can miraculously change your mindset and your day. Those moments are what make your eyes sparkle and people notice that. It's holding your baby's hand for the first time. It's just sitting at the beach quietly listening to the sound of the ocean. Don't worry about the big milestones or the vastness of tasks you need to achieve. Take baby steps! One day at a time. (We will get to time management and setting goals later in the book.)

WHAT IS HAPPINESS?

A key aspect of personal growth is to understand what happiness is.

What does happiness mean to you?

I learnt a valuable lesson about happiness a few years ago, after listening to a great lecture from Fr. Spitzer, who refined the

Four Levels of Happiness model. Today, society teaches us that happiness comes from buying things – from cars to designer clothing. But this is a gross untruth that we have been taught and that we are erroneously teaching future generations.

Level 1 of happiness is immediate gratification, for example, buying a designer handbag. You may feel happy for a few minutes, but it soon wears off.

Level 2 of happiness is personal achievement, but again this is short-lived. It only satisfies your ego, as does Level 1.

We should instead be concentrating on the two highest levels of happiness, Levels 3 and 4.

Level 3 of happiness is contribution. When we contribute to society, to our family, to our friends and to our colleagues, we are doing good beyond our egos, beyond ourselves. We focus our decisions on the common good and this will bring long-term happiness.

Level 4 of happiness is doing the ultimate good. This entails giving and receiving goodness and love. This will give you eternal happiness.

You don't need to watch sci-fi or rom-com movies to step out of reality for a while or to find temporary happiness. You may be a stay-at-home mum right now. Maybe your idiot ex just broke your heart and life looks impossible. But it's not. Your life is amazing. You just need to push through all the negativity. Don't live to escape into movies and books – except this book, of course, and any other book that helps you become better than you are.

Take a deep breath, start being grateful when you wake up, start meditating, go for a walk and, slowly and surely, your days will turn into beautiful weeks, and then beautiful weeks will turn into fabulous years.

I promise you, since I have been practising mindfulness, Levels 3 and 4 of happiness and positive thinking, my life has gone from a 4 out of 10 to a 9.5 out of 10. I'd say 10 out of 10, but I still have to do housework!

If you're in the middle of a tough time, get yourself a support group and face your demons. You can change your life. You can have your cake and eat it too! Don't listen to anyone who tells you otherwise.

When you're *for* yourself and not *against* yourself, you're in agreement with God. Stop being against yourself. There's already enough in this world against you. Think of all the good you do.

> *You can do things with your limitations.*
> *God loves you despite your limitations.*
> *He loved Noah who drank too much…*
> *He loved Peter who lied…*
> *We all have flaws!*

Note to self: I might not be where I want to be but I'm not where I was. I'm no better than anyone else but no one else is better than me. I will put my shoulders back and I am a child of God of the highest.

Nothing about you has been made by accident. You have been faithfully and wonderfully made. The colour of your skin, your limitations, your height, your weight, if you're a girl or a boy – God has already made your path for a reason. You are equipped for the race specifically designed for you.

Remember, Moses didn't want to speak. He even tried to put his brother in front of him to speak, but God said he was equipped.

Think of how a golf ball has dimples. You would think that a very smooth ball would be even better for golf. But, it's *actually* the reverse. The dimples make the ball less wind resistant so it travels further than if it were smooth.

Instead of going around saying, 'So much is wrong with me… I can't speak in public… I'm too scared…I'm not educated enough', try to adopt an attitude of, 'Well, I just have a bunch of dimples and they help me travel further and travel faster. They're not working against me, they're working for me!'

Now that you have some basic tools to lead a positive and happy life, you are armed and ready to start your business.

It might seem simple to keep a routine that helps you stay positive, but if you can discipline yourself to get enough sleep and keep a positive mindset, this will flow through to your business. Don't forget to add to your vision board as you go, and have it somewhere prominent. It's an excellent idea to teach your children and loved ones to have a vision board too.

When you wake up:

1. Express gratitude.
2. Set your intentions for the day.
3. Take five deep breaths in and out.
4. Smile for no reason.
5. Forgive yourself for yesterday's mistakes.

CHAPTER 2
GETTING STARTED

- **SETTING UP**
- **VISION**
- **ACTION PLANS**
- **NETWORKING**
- **CONNECTIONS**

SO, YOU'VE WOKEN UP, it's a new day, you've spent some time being grateful and setting a positive mindset and you're ready to get started! In this chapter, I'm going to cover the key areas that I believe are necessary to start up your business from home.

Remember that you need to keep taking notes and, from time to time, you will need to *stop* reading and go and do some writing or research, and then come back for the next steps.

Take your time and enjoy each step as we progress. Keep your notes in a diary or a notebook so you can go back and reflect on this journey.

SETTING UP

To get started with many aspects of your business, you will need a desktop computer or laptop with Microsoft Office Home & Business software. Consider this a small investment to start up your business. Hopefully, you already have a computer and this software at home, but if you don't, do you know someone who has a laptop they can lend you for a few months? Centrelink is Australia's government support office (if you're outside Australia you'll need to locate your local government support office) and it assists with computer equipment, but make sure they supply you with Microsoft Office Home & Business 365 as well. If not, maybe they can give you a cheap laptop or computer and you can purchase the MS software online at www.microsoft.com.

Please also remember that YouTube is your friend. If you have never used Excel or Word before, simply jump into YouTube and search for 'how to' videos. For example, 'how to use Excel for beginners'. Make yourself a cup of tea, watch some training videos and you'll be using Word and Excel before you know it. The same applies to all areas of this book. YouTube has so much content these days: use it as a training tool. It's free and will help you gain confidence in all areas of business.

Bear in mind that your physical health is just as important as your mental health. Sitting in front of a computer can put strain on your back and neck if you're not sitting properly. Your set-up should look like this (see pictures below). Your screen should be at eye-height and your chair should be of a good design to prevent any back pain or damage.

I slipped a disc in around year three of my business. I was sitting for too long, not taking breaks, and not doing core strengthening exercises. I was still going for a walk on most days and eating and sleeping well, so didn't think I was doing too badly. When I suffered from a slipped disc, I changed my whole routine and set-up at home. I had an excellent physio who spoke to me about my work space, taking frequent breaks and doing small bouts of yoga and other exercises during the day. All it takes is ten minutes, four times a day and I don't suffer from any back pain or further spinal issues.

Please make sure you take care of yourself and, if need be, set an alarm for every two hours to get up and stretch and do a few exercises. When you're sitting down, make sure you are aware of sitting up straight with your shoulders back. Also, you will find that you are a lot more efficient if you can have a double screen set-up – one screen for your emails and another to see other things like databases, or your CRM (customer relationship management) software when you get further established. A second monitor isn't necessary at the start, but you will want to consider getting one a few months into the business.

WHAT WILL YOUR BUSINESS DO?

An early decision you need to make is what the objective is for your new business. What service or product do you want to deliver? Do you want to be the best local hairdresser, or do you want to teach children piano? Do you want to sell art or pottery or clothing that you make? Whatever you want to start up, write down your objective.

Writing your business objective is the very first step to writing a business plan. Don't worry about creating a formal business plan at this stage: that will evolve as your business grows. You don't need a whole business plan when you're just looking to start a small business from home. When I started Credit Fix Solutions, my business objective was to network with local finance brokers to see if I could help their clients with fixing their credit reports. I had a computer from Centrelink and I worked from my son's desk in his bedroom. You don't need to invest in lengthy business programs or courses at this stage either, and, if you are in a low financial position as I was, you won't have the money for them anyway.

If you follow this book, you will have all the tools to set up your business from home and start making some money – then you can go and do a business course. I recommend a specific business course at the end of the book.

VISION

Vision is important to you right now, and forever more in your business, as it's what people will follow you for. If you can clearly explain your vision for your business, your passion will show through, and people will want to do business with you. People will want to work for you, and they will help you achieve your vision. It's human nature for people to want to be part of a business that will have an impact and is going somewhere. Even if it remains a small, family-run business, if you have vision and passion, people will want to work with you and clients will be happy to part with their hard-earned cash.

Take some time now to think about your vision and *write it down*. Stick it up on your vision board and every few months sit down and rethink your vision. Your vision will grow or change with your business.

Our vision

Our vision at Credit Fix Solutions is to be the market-leading credit repair and debt negotiation service in Australia, offering the best value, fast and friendly, no-result no-fee advocacy services to our customers to help them and their families improve their financial future.

When I started six years ago, my vision was different of course. Back then, my vision was just to focus on helping local finance brokers to fix their clients' credit reports on a no-result no-fee basis. And that was fine at the time. I was incredibly happy with the small business I had created. I've just evolved with the business as it's grown and so our vision has changed.

In order to work out if your business is relevant and could potentially be an income-earner, you need to go and research the market you are looking at entering. Ask yourself why you think your business is relevant today, and how it will be relevant in five years' time. What are your potential competitors doing? What are they not doing well? Is there a niche that competitors haven't filled that you could fill with a local business? If you're comfortable that there is a niche in the local market that you can fill, and it's a service or product that people will want in the future, then go for it!

WHAT WILL YOU CALL YOUR BUSINESS?

Now you need to think of a business name and register it, apply for an ABN (Australian Business Number) and domain name (this is the name you give your website). I remember being so excited when I came up with my business name and registered it so that I could get my ABN.

It's best to work out your business name before you start creating marketing material, or your website, or printing business cards, etc. Otherwise, if you change your business name, you'll have to go back and change everything. (See chapter 8 to find out how to register your business name and apply for an ABN and then jump back to here once you're done. I've covered Australia, the UK and the US in chapter 8.)

To check whether the name you'd like for your website is available (in Australia), go to the domain name registry www.netregistry.com.au/get-started/establish-my-brand. If you're in a different country, you can look up your government website, which will have information and instructions for how to set up a business name and the legal aspects you will be required to comply with. (You will learn about setting up your website later in the book.)

If you have no idea what business name to pick, you'll need to jump ahead to chapter 3 and create your avatar and brand identity. Then you can come back and register your domain name before getting into your action planning.

CREATING YOUR ACTION PLAN

Now you have your business name and ABN, let's get to your action plan!

When I started in business, I thought I had to have a huge plan and long-term goals. This can be quite overwhelming – and is not the case. The secret to starting your business is to work towards daily goals on five items or projects you would like to complete over the next three months. Then in three months' time, you simply start the whole cycle again.

This idea was suggested to me by Business Blueprint, which I highly recommend you look into once you've started your business and you need some business training. (Their website is businessblueprint.com.au. Further details are given in the final chapter.)

For example, when I first started my business, I looked three months ahead, and I wrote down five things I would like to achieve:

1. Networking
2. Lead generation
3. Social media posting
4. Website/email
5. Business cards and flyers.

Whatever business you are starting, what would be five things you can do in the next three months?

Write those five things down.

Then work on those five things every day, even if it's only for 30 minutes per item.

You'll be amazed that within a few weeks you will be nearly halfway to completing the five items on your list.

Then in three months' time, you should have completed the items and you can think of your next five items for the following three months. Easy!!

Example initial business start-up action plan

90-day action plan

1. Organise serviced office.
   - Research local serviced offices.
   - Go in and have a look at the offices.
   - Look at the location for ease of parking/meetings.
2. Set up basic website.
   - Research website designers in your area or on Fiverr.com.
   - Research Wordpress designs and pick one.
3. Organise email and signature.
   - Create a Gmail email account.
   - Create a signature (which will include your name, business name and phone number).
4. Design logo.
   - Get a designer on Fiverr.com to design some logo ideas.
   - Research competitors' designs.
   - Think about colour and fonts.
5. Print business cards.
   - Finalise your logo.
   - Decide upon your title. Will you be 'CEO', 'Founder' or use your occupation as your title, e.g. 'Accountant', 'Hairdresser'?
   - Organise a virtual office address and phone number.
   - Find a designer on Fiverr.com to design your business card.

Once you have your three-month plan, write your five daily goals in your notepad and every day tick next to each goal when you've worked on it.

Rewarding yourself is also important!

As motivation to help you complete your goals, you need to have a reward in mind. Underneath each goal, I want you to write your completion date (when you aim to achieve this goal), then write next to that your personal reward. Here's an example:

Example

1. Organise serviced office space
   Completion date: 30 June 2021
   Personal reward: Spa day

At the end of the day, if you have given your best, at least you can say you gave it a go! Try and, if you fail, try harder.

NETWORKING AND MAKING CONNECTIONS

When you have created a basic website, printed your business cards and started posting on social media, it's time to start networking in your local area. Irrespective of which industry you are entering, there will be networks you can join which will offer support. If you have a hairdressing business, there may be a great women's networking group in your town, for example. Why not go along and network with the women in that group? Of course, don't throw your business card in their face. Simply try to connect with five to ten people at a networking function, and then try to arrange a follow-up coffee meeting with them individually.

If you connect with 10 people a week at events, that's 40 people you can potentially do business with every month – and 120 people in the first three months! This is how I grew my business when I started. I joined local business groups, created relationships, met with the same people on a regular basis and, in three months, I had established nearly 100 referral partners who were sending me clients.

Another way to connect with other business owners is via a business association. In Australia, a great association that offers access to programs, services, technology, quality education and support for small businesses is the Small Business Association of Australia (www.smallbusinessassociation.com.au).

If you live elsewhere, I'm sure you have some great options for a supportive business association that you can join.

Lead generation is a broad topic and there are many ways to create leads to start filling your sales funnel. Networking is a great way to generate leads. The only real cost is your time, but you can also use other methods – for example, online. Some businesses run ads on Facebook, but you need money to do this. Others use LinkedIn, which offers limited free access that worked for me. I created a profile on LinkedIn and started adding people whom I thought I could do business with. Then I sent them a private message asking them if they would like to have a coffee. Out of every ten messages I'd send, around four people would say yes. Then I would arrange a meeting and keep doing this every week.

Create your LinkedIn profile today. You only need a personal account. As I said, it's free, and you can then add people every day who potentially could benefit from your product or service. Your target is to add 20 relevant people to your LinkedIn profile every day. Then you send a private message to whoever connects and suggest you catch up for a coffee (at their office, or a local coffee shop is fine) and start building a relationship.

I now have more than 15,000 relevant connections on LinkedIn – and I started with zero. There is no secret to building your connections. Just consistently add people every day and then send them messages via LinkedIn to catch up. You will learn who your target customers and/or referrers are in chapter 3.

Consistency is the key when sending messages out on LinkedIn. Keep connecting with 20 new people a day – don't stop! When you meet with people in person, make sure that you are *adding value to their business* or the meeting in general.

I want you also to start commenting on and liking posts from your connections on LinkedIn. There are groups on LinkedIn that you can join too. Make sure you comment on posts from others in the group or post content yourself for the group on a regular basis. This will help establish yourself as a 'go-to' person in your industry. It will keep you front of mind for your online audience.

You can grow your network in a similar way using Facebook. If you don't have a Facebook account, make sure you create one and start adding people who may be interested in your new product or service. Maybe you're going to provide home cooking in your local area. Why not connect with other mums or dads from your children's school? Or start adding people once you have connected with them through LinkedIn or your networking events?

Consistency is key to everything you do, from your personal life through to your work. (We go through social media and how to post content in chapter 5.)

Are there events that you can go to where you could network as well? I know that networking may seem a little daunting but, if you introduce yourself to someone and then focus on learning something about them by asking them questions, I find that this helps create a connection and breaks the ice. Once you've connected, they will ask what you do and you can tell them about yourself.

Have a 60-second pitch ready. For example, I would say, 'I help people improve their credit scores and save them thousands of dollars on interest rates.' Write a few ideas down for your 60-second pitch now and try them out on family and friends. You'll soon find one that works, that creates interest and conversation. (See chapter 3 for more information on creating a 60-second pitch.)

It's most important that you follow up with people you've met, as you need to stay front of mind. I used Mailchimp to do this at first. Mailchimp is a free basic client management system. Go and check it out. It allows you to compile a database of contacts and send them email blasts (these are called EDMs or electronic direct mail) all in one hit, or according to their profiles. Make sure you segregate your lists according to client profiles as much as you can from the start. For example, if we run an event in Sydney, I don't want to email my referral partners in Perth. So, I have segmented our lists by geographical area.

Sending boring salesy emails is not advisable. With your email blasts and social media posts, make sure you are being educational or at least positive and helpful.

All our social media posts are focused on our audience. If we are sending a post out to consumers, for example on Facebook, we may send something out like, *'Did you know you have three credit reports and each can contain different information?'* This creates interest and builds trust with our audience, and we're not trying to sell them anything. Focus your marketing strategy on being a source of education and you won't fail.

Think about your audience. What is helpful to them? What is educational? Do you have a special offer for them? Have a look at our Credit Fix Solutions Facebook page (www.facebook.com/creditfixsolutions) for ideas on social media posting. Social media and marketing are covered in more depth in chapter 5.

We talk more about building your website in chapter 6, but I want to mention here that your first website only needs to be a simple, one-page website with a contact form. The contact form should ask for the person's name, email address and mobile number – that way you can add them to your database of contacts. Then you can send them a quick email and take the contact from there.

Make sure that the website is a WordPress website, which is easy to log into and alter text or add pages later. You don't want a website built with code, because you will always need a website designer or developer to go in and make changes.

Have a look at WordPress website designs online and pick one you like before engaging someone on Fiverr.com to create your design. We also encourage using local businesses in your area to help you – as long as they aren't ripping you off! We use a few local businesses to help us with various aspects of Credit Fix Solutions, and it's important that we help our local business owners and our economy.

Use Word to type up your website pages before sending these to your website designer. Think about your content being customer-facing. In business, we tend to send messages out to potential clients that we understand, but you need to think about what the person looking at your website wants to read. *Are you connecting to the person looking at your website?*

Have a look at websites of existing competitors to get some ideas.

Get your website, business card and email set up, and you're ready to network or get your first clients in!

Your website will grow as you bring in more business, and then you can add to it. There's no need to spend thousands of dollars now when you haven't even earnt a cent! I ordered 100 business cards from Vistaprint (www.vistaprint.com.au) when I first started. I think they cost me around $50 and this was a great way to get out there and promote our services.

Vistaprint provides designs for your marketing material as well, so you can use one of their preprepared designs, without even going to Fiverr to get a cheap design for your logo.

Remember, people will want to do business with you *because of you*, not because you have an amazing logo or marketing material!

WHAT ABOUT AN OFFICE?

Despite this book being aimed at people starting a business from home, if you are looking to provide a professional service, consider whether you will need an office. You must make this decision before you print your business cards. Alternatively, you can rent a post office box and give that as your contact address, rather than a physical address.

Don't freak out! When I first started my business from my son's bedroom, there was no way that I could afford office space. Also, I hadn't even started networking, so asking another business owner to share their space wasn't going to happen. I investigated serviced office spaces in Parramatta and researched a few options. I chose a company that provided me with an address, a phone number and a receptionist to answer calls for around $200 per month. This is a great way to start your business. It looks professional to the general public and for a small monthly fee, you have an address and phone number to print on your business card immediately.

Obviously, serviced office providers are looking to make money. So, they charge high fees if you want to book an office for a meeting. I couldn't afford this early on, so if a client or potential referral partner wanted to meet at the office, I'd book the meeting with them and arrange to meet them in the ground-floor coffee shop. This meant we were (in theory) still at my office, but the cost of the meeting was only the price of a coffee! In fact, I still do this today, unless I need to book the boardroom. What's the point of using an office for $50 to $100 per meeting when you can simply buy someone a coffee for around $10 for the both of you!

This chapter is a summary of getting started. Don't worry if you feel you need more information, as we go into details in the chapters to come.

WHAT ABOUT AN OFFICE?

Despite this book being aimed at people starting a business from home, if you are looking to provide a professional service, consider whether you will need an office. You must make this decision before you print your business cards. Alternatively, you can rent a post office box and give that as your contact address, rather than a physical address.

Don't freak out! When I first started my business from my son's bedroom, there was no way that I could afford office space. Also, I hadn't even started networking, so asking another business owner to share their space wasn't going to happen. I investigated serviced office spaces in Parramatta and researched a few options. I chose a company that provided me with an address, a phone number and a receptionist to answer calls for around $200 per month. This is a great way to start your business. It looks professional to the general public and for a small monthly fee, you have an address and phone number to print on your business card immediately.

Obviously, serviced office providers are looking to make money. So, they charge high fees if you want to book an office for a meeting. I couldn't afford this early on, so if a client or potential referral partner wanted to meet at the office, I'd book the meeting with them and arrange to meet them in the ground-floor coffee shop. This meant we were (in theory) still at my office, but the cost of the meeting was only the price of a coffee! In fact, I still do this today, unless I need to book the boardroom. What's the point of using an office for $50 to $100 per meeting when you can simply buy someone a coffee for around $10 for the both of you!

This chapter is a summary of getting started. Don't worry if you feel you need more information, as we go into details in the chapters to come.

CHAPTER 3
FINDING YOUR TARGET CUSTOMERS

- **CREATING YOUR AVATAR**
- **FINDING AND DOMINATING YOUR MARKET POSITION**

WHEN CREATING YOUR WEBSITE and other marketing material for your start-up business, it's vital that you understand who your target customer is.

This chapter may look quite short, but it will get you to do a lot of thinking and researching and writing as you work through it. The reading is the easy part! It's *action time* now!

Creating your 'client/referrer avatar' is the first step in getting to know your ideal client or target customer. In marketing, an avatar is a little fiction or story that helps you understand your ideal client, target customer or the person who is going to refer you business, so you can more easily find them. Let's start with an emotional and physical description – an avatar – of your ideal client and/or referrer. I want you to stop at this point and write down some key emotional and physical features of your avatar:

- Are they female or male?
- What is their age?
- What are their interests?
- What are they thinking or how are they feeling? Purchasing behaviour is almost solely drive by emotion. Understanding how your customer thinks and feels will have a huge impact on how you market to them, your branding and how your sales strategies are developed.
- Where do they live?
- What are their psychographics (their emotional make-up)?

- What level of customer service and/or pricing will your avatar be happy with?
- What levels of convenience do you need to offer (e.g. location, availability, ordering process, delivery, payment terms, miscellaneous services)?
- What levels of speed of services or products do you provide and will your customer be happy with this?
- What education or training do they have?
- What is/are the perceived benefit(s) of your product or service to them?
- What security and safety are they expecting (e.g. online safety)?
- What pricing is fair?

When you have written down a detailed description of your target customers, you will have the fundamental information you need to communicate with them through your marketing. You will know the language you need to use when speaking and dealing with potential customers and/or referral partners. This works in B2C (business to consumer) marketing and B2B (business to business).

FIVE-STEP DIFFERENTIATION PROCESS

You now need to create your market-dominating position: your brand identity. To do this, go through each of the five steps below and write down your answers as you go.

1. **Strategic position** – Define your businesses product and/or service offering/s.

Example: No-result no-fee credit report and debt improvement services.

2. **Primary market-dominating position** – What's the main thing you will do?

    Example: Consulting on credit report improvement and debt minimisation solutions.

3. **Secondary market-dominating position** – Are there add-ons that you can provide?

    Example: Free consultation/access to eBook/free credit reports with consultation.

4. **Supporting business model** – This will be just you for now, until your business becomes more established.

    Example: A BDM (business development manager)/staff with basic planning and credit reporting knowledge, who have had specialised training.

5. **Your 60-second elevator pitch** – Your 60-second pitch is how you sell yourself to other people. We'll discuss this in more detail below.

DRAFTING YOUR 60-SECOND ELEVATOR PITCH

Your elevator pitch must be short and catchy. Ask yourself the following questions and then start putting your elevator pitch together:

- What is the purpose of your business or organisation?
- What do you do and why does it matter?

Also consider what is unique about your business, i.e. what makes it stand out from your competitors?

You need to spend time on this; and remember, you can bounce your ideas off local business owners and friends you've made through networking.

HOW TO SPEAK TO YOUR AVATAR

You need to be mindful when selling. Answering the following three questions should help you shape the way that you speak to your target customers. Remember to add these to your vision board today!

1. What do you do to solve their problem?
2. What do you do that makes them more money?
3. What do you do that is strengthening their business?

Here's my example:

> I specialise in educating people about their credit reports. I help to remove bad credit and manage debts for people to improve their financial future to benefit themselves and their families and businesses. Credit Fix Solutions offers fast and friendly, no-result no-fee credit repair and debt negotiation services Australia-wide. We help people improve their lives by helping them remove unfair listings from their credit reports and negotiating debts on their behalf so they can move forward with the finances they need for their families.

Now go and review your answers, following the examples I have given above, and you will be reading your very first brand identity!

Another great add-on, when you are creating a market-dominating position, is to offer an instant quote with no lock-in contacts if you can.

Perhaps you can offer a selection of add-on services, for example:

- An eBook priced at $29.95
- A free credit report with consultation
- A free initial consultation
- An instant report and score for $49.95.

Now you have your avatar(s) and your ideas for creating a market-dominating position (brand identity). In the next chapter we are going to cover systems and data management. These are important components in establishing and running a successful start-up.

BTW, congratulations on completing the first three chapters! Go back and review how far you've come and give yourself a reward! Well done! You've just taken the first steps in your business start-up!

CHAPTER 4
MANAGING YOUR SYSTEMS

- **BUILDING YOUR DATABASE**
- **MANAGING YOUR CALENDAR**
- **TIME MANAGEMENT**

HAVING A PILE of manila folders stacked on your desk with all your clients' histories is not a great system.

I've been to some referral partner offices over the years and seen Post-it Notes and folders everywhere. They seem to have no idea where or how to start their day, or in what order to arrange their tasks – or even what is high-priority each day when they start work. This is common for micro businesses, when there may be just one person running the show.

It's not a habit that you want to start, because it's easy to get into and hard to get out of.

As I discussed in chapter 1, it is vital to have order in your day on a personal level, and to be consistent, if you are to become the best version of yourself. The same applies to running your business, and this starts with your database management and how you set up your systems. It is of the utmost importance to learn how to use software, then apply the same daily order and consistency to your business life if you are to grow a successful business.

People who get stuck on systems focus too much on the 'in the business' tasks and they fail to work on improving their 'on the business' skills. This is no way to start your business venture. The more good systems, procedures, workflows and project management tools that you learn and use, the easier your workload will be, and the more your business will flourish.

To be honest, when I started, I had no idea about these systems or working 'on the business'. I had stacks of client folders, and I had to manually go through all the folders every morning to gauge which of them I had to work on that day. It makes me laugh to think of all the time I wasted.

I had to learn by speaking to other business owners with whom I had connected and asking them how they managed their databases, etc., and scraping together ideas as I went. This is not ideal, and I don't want you to start in this fashion. You should already have your plan of action of how you are going to get business in the door, but how do you manage those new leads?

DATABASE MANAGEMENT

Database management allows you to organise, store and retrieve data from your computer. It allows you to segment your lists of clients and potential clients, assign tasks as needed and send out emails to people as you see fit.

More expensive database management systems, or CRM (customer relationship management) systems, will give you integrated software solutions that can improve how you interact and do business with your customers. CRM systems will also help you manage and maintain your relationships with your customers, track sales and leads, and help with automation and marketing.

We currently use a CRM system called Ontraport. It took time to add our existing data and several years to learn how to get the best use out of Ontraport. But as time-consuming as it was, we now have a superb CRM system that allows us to track and record everything – from leads through to referral partners to automation of tasks – it's very exciting! If you're interested in Ontraport, you can check it out at www.ontraport.com.

However, I didn't start with Ontraport, and if you're starting your business with no money, as I did, then you can begin by using basic database systems. When you get to the end of your first year in business, then I suggest you do a business course (see my recommendations at the end of this book) so you can learn how to implement a more complicated CRM system into your business – but you don't need it now.

To begin with, however, there are a few more basic database system options that you can investigate. You can create temporary accounts with the following for free:

- Pipedrive
- Mailchimp
- Zoho.

Before you panic about setting up and using CRM or database software, which can be confusing, don't worry! You can simply work off Excel spreadsheets to start with and use your calendar to log meetings, calls and any tasks if you feel that a CRM system is beyond your skill level at this stage.

Fun Fact: Do you know what 'to excel' means in the dictionary? It's a verb meaning, 'to be exceptionally good at or proficient in an activity or subject'.

As its name denotes, Microsoft Excel will help you to proficiently manage your data, sales and reporting for your business. Excel's features include calculation, graphing tools and pivot tables. It's super easy to use and you can set up spreadsheets with little help or study.

A few reports/databases that you could immediately set up are:

- A leads report
- A customer/client database
- A sales report
- An invoices-out report
- A referral partner database
- A business income and expenses (see chapter 8).

Let's look at how to set these up in Excel now.

SETTING UP YOUR DATABASES AND REPORTS

For leads, customer and referral partner databases, you need to create a few columns. Make sure you have all their relevant contact details, including first name, last name, phone number, email, unit number, street number and name, suburb, state and postcode.

The reason I suggest splitting the data like this on your spreadsheet is because later, if you move to a CRM system, exporting the data will be a dream!

A basic Excel client or customer spreadsheet can be set up like the example below:

You can also use Excel to keep a tidy list of your sales, as in the example below:

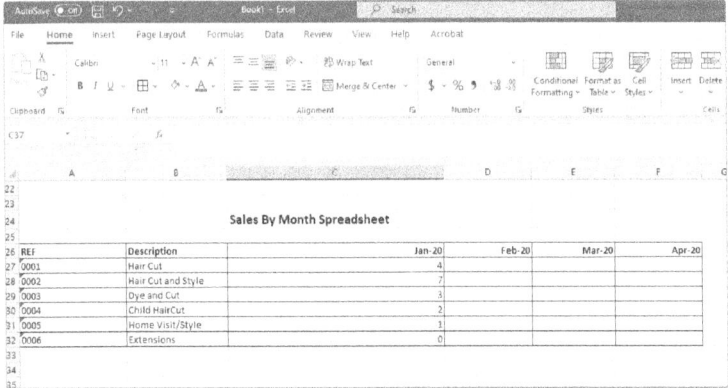

MANAGING YOUR SYSTEMS 53

Once you have Excel and your calendar organised, then you can create a Mailchimp account (we discussed Mailchimp in chapter 2). You can then import your customer or referrer data from Excel to Mailchimp and send out email blasts to your contacts for marketing purposes.

(In the next chapter we discuss social media platforms and posting; email marketing is covered in chapter 6.)

CALENDAR MANAGEMENT

Calendar management is also easy to set up. We use Gmail and then use the related Google Calendar. Don't worry about having your own email server for now. But if you think you can set up a server and have your emails come through to your Gmail account, then go for it! Gmail is great because it allows you to use Google Drive to electronically store your client files, databases, etc., and you can use your Google Calendar to add meetings, events, and reminders. It's easy to set up Gmail and your Google Calendar on your phone too, and your phone will sync with your computer, making life a little simpler.

APPLICATION FORMS

If you use application forms in your business (perhaps you run a service that requires you to have a privacy form signed by a customer as per legislation), then you'll need to create these.

Creating an application form and getting it out to customers may seem daunting. (I go through the legal side of applications in chapter 8, where I cover your privacy policy and other terms and conditions.)

How do people sign up with your business or purchase from you? Years ago, I had to print off our application form and meet people face to face to sign them up. It was time-consuming and tiring! With today's technology, we have an electronic application platform, which allows us to pre-fill an application form, and then we use another company, SignRequest, to electronically send out the application for signing.

SignRequest is free to start with and then, as you need to use more features or send out more documents, their pricing is competitive. Their site sends email reminders to clients to sign the applications, and once we get the applications back in, we can easily start work and save their signed application to our Google Drive.

You can create a basic application form in Word and then save a PDF copy, or you could ask someone at Fiverr.com to create a basic PDF application for you. You can then save a blank PDF copy of your application form to your computer/Google Drive/OneDrive. This means that when you are speaking to a customer over the phone, or in person, you can complete the PDF with them. (Adobe software creates PDFs which are easy to fill electronically.) Then save the completed form to your computer (we have a leads folder in Google Drive, and we create a folder in there which is where we save the unsigned application). You can later upload the completed application to SignRequest and select the fields you need your client to sign and then trigger for the application to be emailed to them for signature. For more information on SignRequest, go to www.signrequest.com/ref/7WQVKY9Z.

I would like to point out that you will not be able to continue to use basic systems such as Excel, Mailchimp and your

Calendar for long. They will assist you when you are starting up, but at some point within six to twelve months, if your business has grown, you will want to get a more full-featured CRM software package. I would also recommend that you consider joining a business coaching group.

For future reference, the one and only group for Australia that I would ever recommend joining is Business Blueprint, as mentioned earlier, which was developed by Dale Beaumont and his team. Details are in the final chapter if you would like to attend one of Dale's free introductory sessions.

Around 12 months into my business, we had around 50 clients at any one time. I had a part-time assistant and I was drowning in paperwork and basic systems.

So, I went along to one of Dale's introductory days. He has them running all over Australia if you're interested. In that one day alone, I was able to take away a few new tools to implement in my business, and so I joined their 12-month program. If you're outside Australia, search business development courses and do your research.

Now I was in *no way* making a lot of money. However, I realised that unless I invested in myself, I would not be able to run a rapidly growing company. So, although it wasn't easy to pay the monthly costs, I decided that I would focus 200 per cent on the course and implement as much as I could. By the time I completed the course, a year later, my revenue had doubled, I had implemented a CRM and other systems, and I had learned how to use other tools to grow my business.

TIME MANAGEMENT

The last system I want to teach you about is your time management system. If you spend all week out at events or networking, when will you have time to create content, or work on other areas of your business?

For the first year or two, I worked seven days a week, but I made time during the week for 'me time', as well as ensuring there were days when I didn't have meetings. If you push yourself too hard, you will burn out and, more importantly, you could lose your passion for creating something special.

Get your week's calendar in front of you. What do you need to do every week? When do you have appointments? When can you make time to schedule your social media posting? Make sure you include 'me time' a few times a week – and times when you stop doing anything work related, and simply have some family time.

When I was starting out, I found that a good way to structure the week was to have Monday and Fridays as admin days (when I stayed at home in my PJs and worked on marketing material and blogging – 'on the business' tasks). Then I scheduled meetings, webinars, etc. for Tuesday, Wednesday and Thursday. Once a month I had a day when I created written content for the following four weeks, and I made sure that at least one day a week I did nothing and spent time with family and friends or just chilling out watching movies.

Now we are a national company with over 10 staff and my weeks are a bit different, but I remember the above structure working well for me when the business was smaller.

If you're thinking of selling goods online, it can be a bit of a headache to work out integrations on websites with forms and banks, etc. We don't sell online, but a great business tool I have come across for you can be found at www.squareup.com/au/en/online-store. Square offers a simple solution for you to easily create an online platform to sell goods. And you don't pay any fees until you make a sale!

So, for now, you will be starting your business using this book as a mentoring guide, but if it starts to grow outside of your skill set, please use the link at the end of this book to subscribe for a complimentary introductory day with Business Blueprint.

CHAPTER 5
A STEP-BY-STEP GUIDE TO SOCIAL MEDIA

- **SOCIAL MEDIA PLATFORMS**
- **USING HOOTSUITE**

Screenshots supplied by Hootsuite and used with their permission.

SO, NOW YOU HAVE worked on yourself, your vision, your messaging, networking and your systems, and you have set up your social media accounts (on LinkedIn and Facebook). You have created your avatar, and hopefully printed some marketing material.

The question now is, 'How do I get my product or service out there to my online audience?'

You may be meeting referral partners or networking at events selling your products and services, but it is imperative that you are front of mind as much as possible so that existing referral partners and clients don't forget about you *and* so you can get in front of potential new customers and/or referral partners.

In this chapter, we will cover social media posting, and you can follow an easy step-by-step guide to using Hootsuite to load up social media messages for the week. I used to panic about posting on social media: 'What do I post? Will I remember every day to post? Am I too busy working in the business to think about "on the business" tasks?'

A social media posting platform like Hootsuite is a great way for you to set and forget your posts for the week, in one weekly session, by scheduling the days and times you want your posts to go out across your social media accounts.

At Credit Fix Solutions and Credit Fix Lawyers, we use Hootsuite for our social media posting. There are other platforms that you can research and use, but I'm going to use Hootsuite as a guide for the purposes of training in this book.

If it's just you using the platform, and you've got fewer than three social profiles, then this platform is free for a trial period.

Of course, you still need to be organised. I spend an hour every Monday loading the week's posts across all our social profiles. We have ten, so we pay $39 per month, but it's worth it. Before you post you need to consider:

- Are there any events coming up that you could post about? Valentine's Day, Christmas, etc.? Or economic events, COVID-19, an election?
- How does your post help your audience?
- Are there any special offers that you can post?

We have an educational focus on social media posting and it works. Don't be salesy, because you won't connect with your audience. If you are educational, your audience will feel valued and will be more likely to connect with you. I'll show you some post ideas soon to give you some insight about what posts should look like.

I suggest you follow this system to organise your posting session for the week:

1. Sit down and think about any events that are coming up that week.
2. Think about what you can post that will be of value to your audience.
3. Select your images before you log into Hootsuite, so you are ready to post.

You will need to select and save your images before you start a new post. We use Shutterstock (www.shutterstock.com), so we pay for images, and then I save them to our Shutterstock folder. You could visit www.pixabay.com, where you can download free images for commercial use, but be careful using photos you source from the internet for free because of copyright issues – not many images are royalty-free for commercial use. We use Shutterstock because I find there is more variety and they have a great editing tool, so I can add websites, addresses and text to the photos, and other stuff too if I want.

Right, we're ready now to go to the Hootsuite website at www.hootsuite.com and sign up. Once you're at the website, click on the green 'Sign Up' button to create your account.

You can choose to opt in for four months free, and then you will pay roughly AU$40 per month after that. Getting the first four months free is great! You will be able to set up your networks with Facebook or LinkedIn, for example, in this time, and have an audience to market to.

When you've signed up and created an account you will be able to log in. Then you'll be guided to set up social accounts. When you've added accounts (and eventually some posts), your home screen will look like this:

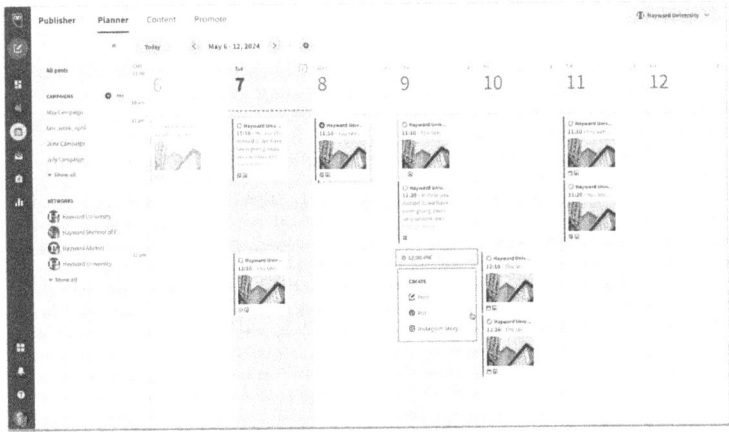

Every time you log in, you'll be automatically taken to the 'Streams' tab. (The icon that looks like four squares together is the Streams tab and the word 'Streams' pops up when you hover your mouse over this icon.) If you look on the left-hand side of the screenshot, you will see your tab options.

For now, you only need to worry about the 'Create Post' button and the 'Inbox' and 'Publisher' tabs. When you hover over the 'Inbox' icon, the word 'Inbox' pops up. When you hover over the Calendar icon, the word 'Publisher' pops up and you click on the icon. The other tabs are for advanced users, and you don't need to use them yet. Later on, in a few months' to a year's time, hopefully you'll be running a successful start-up, and then you can do business courses to help you with the advanced features. For now, I just want you to be able to start posting across your social media networks.

We're not going to get into Facebook advertising or any paid advertising yet. This is something you will do later when you've earnt some money, and you have some cash to use for training on courses related to advertising online.

If you haven't set up your social media networks, you will need to do this first (although I know most of you will be working alongside this book and will have set up these accounts already as I suggested!). Of course, if you don't have any followers on your social media accounts you won't have an audience to post to. So, make sure you add people to your networks before you start posting. Then keep inviting potential clients or referral partners to connect with you on your social networks moving forward, so you can start engaging them with your posts.

As I said earlier, when I started my business, I created a personal LinkedIn page and then, every day, I searched people who I thought would be interested in our services, and I added them. Every day I added 20 to 40 people in the finance sector in Australia. Sometimes I did this while queuing at the supermarket checkout, other times I did it while watching crap on TV in the evenings.

It's so easy, but the secret is to do this consistently, every day.

Now, five years on, I have over 15,000 contacts, all relevant to our services. On average, I get around two to five leads per week just from LinkedIn. We have several accounts on Hootsuite and posting to them only costs me a few dollars every week.

For the first couple of years, before I had staff to post for me, I got leads from there for free every week! You can too! Make adding people to your social networks a daily task.

You have a few social media options to choose from. We use Facebook, LinkedIn, Twitter and Instagram, but feel free to choose the networks that will serve your business best.

The screenshot on the previous page shows what your 'Streams' tab looks like when you've added your social networks. To add a social network, simply click the '+ Add Social Network' button and follow the prompts. You will have to log into each network to allow Hootsuite access, to allow the system to post on your behalf.

Now let's go to the 'Inbox' tab and have a look. Click on the Inbox button on the left-hand side tab.

The Inbox tab is a great feature of Hootsuite: it loads up any comments or messages you've received from any social media accounts that you have connected to your account. Rather than having to separately keep on checking your social media accounts in case someone has sent you a message, your messages for any connected account will automatically populate in your Inbox. This means you have just one platform that you need to keep an eye on for any messages. These messages could be important – enquiries for your service or maybe a request for information. The Inbox will not only be a great time-saver for you when you're reading your comments, but it allows you to reply to messages quickly too.

In sales, you have about a 10- to 20-minute window to reply to enquiries, before your conversion rates drop severely. If you reply to an enquiry within 10 minutes you have around an 80 per cent chance to convert the lead; a 60-minute delay drops your conversion rate to around 20 per cent. Be quick and don't let your competitors beat you to it! By using Hootsuite, you can keep your Inbox open during working hours, giving you peace of mind that you can see all enquiries as they come through in real-time.

HOW TO CREATE A POST

Now, let's look at how you create a post. This is a step-by-step process, so I'm hoping it's super-easy to follow. When you're in your Streams tab, you simply click 'New Post'.

When you've clicked 'New Post', you'll be taken to the next screen – the New Post edit screen.

First, you add the social networks that you are going to post to (LinkedIn, Facebook, Twitter, etc.).

Then simply click your mouse in the box that says 'Select a Social Network' and the system will ask you to select the social networks to post to. Next, an area on the right-hand side will populate.

So, from the screenshot below of our Hootsuite account, you can see what our post is going to look like – in this example, on our Twitter page. This is great, because you can gauge what your image and post will look like before you decide to post.

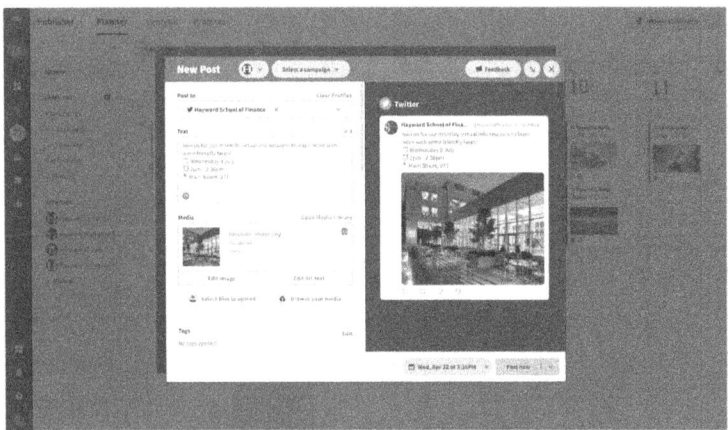

Now, you're going to scroll down to the text section (on the left-hand side) and start typing your post.

As you type in the box on the left-hand side, the text will automatically populate on the right-hand side.

Keep your message short and to the point. Remember to be educational in order to connect to your audience. I will share some social media post examples shortly.

Now you have added your text, scroll down further to the media section to add in your image.

Earlier in the chapter, I mentioned that you need to think about your messages for the week first and save your images before you start adding your posts on Hootsuite.

You should have saved your images already but, if you haven't, go and do this and come back to Hootsuite.

Once you have your saved images, select the file from your computer. Your image will populate to show you what it looks like in your post (as in the screenshot on the previous page).

Now, it's time to schedule your post. Bearing in mind that you are setting a full week's worth of posts, you'll choose the 'Schedule for Later' option. The date box will pop up and you can choose your date and time.

We don't post on Mondays. I've completed business courses on social media posting and, the rule of thumb for business-to-business posting is to post on Tuesday, Wednesday, Thursday and Friday between 10am and 2pm. However, this works for us – maybe your audience is on Facebook in the evenings. Gauge your responses every week and look out for spikes in views or likes or messages, and as you start posting regularly you will work out the best days and times to post.

Select your date and time, and then click 'Schedule'.

And, hey presto! You've just created your first post, *well done!*

If you now click on the 'Publisher' button (Calendar icon) in the left-hand side tab, you will be able to see your scheduled content, as per the image opposite.

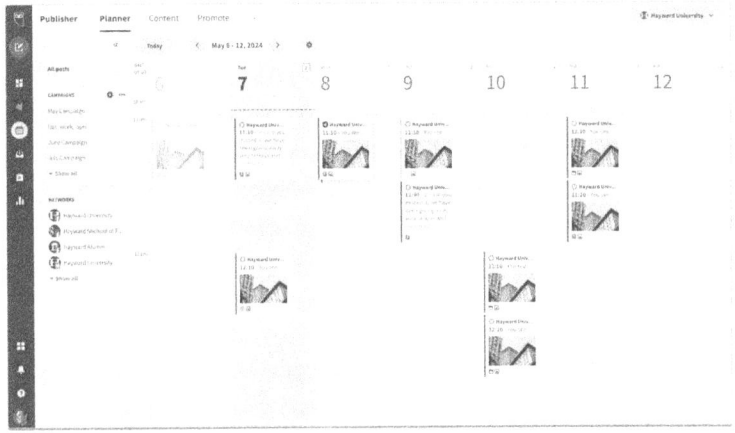

SOCIAL MEDIA POST EXAMPLES

Now let's look at some social media post examples.

Keeping in line with our rules for social media posting, in the first example following, we have a short educational message.

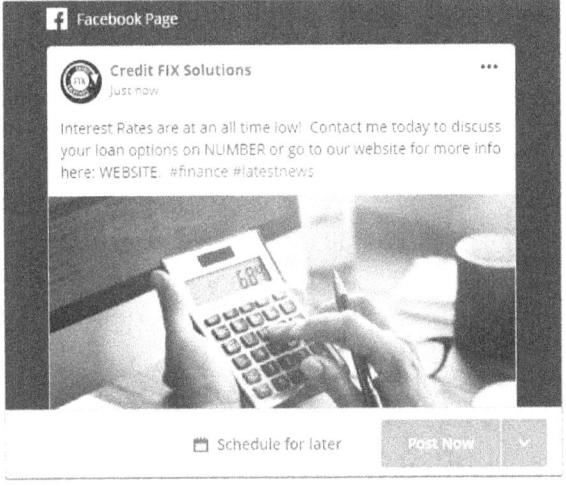

Our image relates to our message and we have placed our phone number and website as a call to action (CTA) on the post. If you haven't set up your website already, you can put your email address as your CTA instead. But make sure you have your CTA! How else are people going to contact you?

In the second social media post example (below), our message is short and educational with a relevant CTA and image.

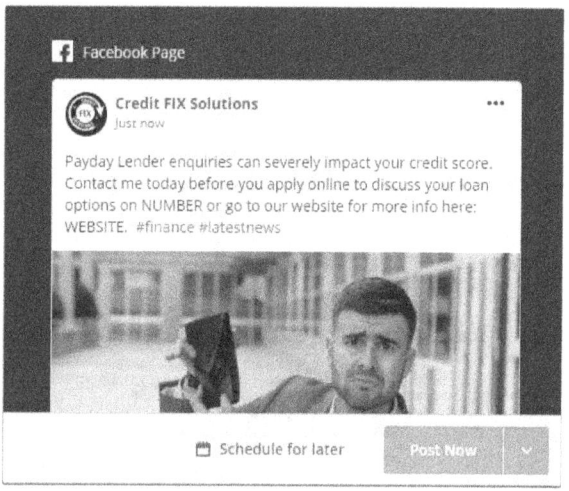

Don't be afraid to use funny images, as we have here. Also, don't make your message too long, as people won't scroll through their feed and find the 'Read More' to read your whole message. Make sure your audience can quickly scan your entire message without having to click the 'Read More' option to maximise your conversion potential.

In our third social media post example, we've used a bright and colourful image to catch a person's attention.

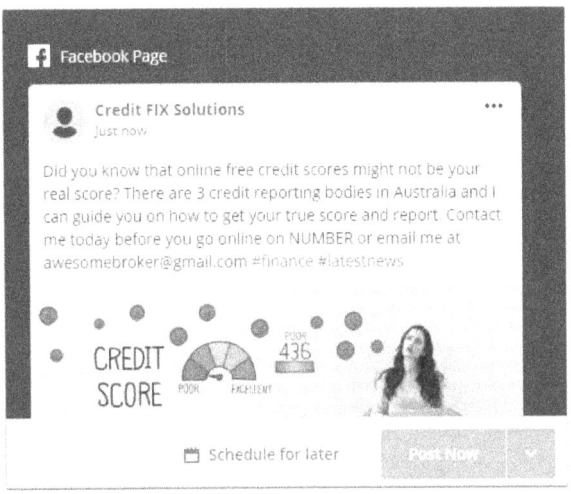

Think about how your audience relates to the image you are using. With this image, we are thinking about all the wives sitting at home on social media, wondering about finance. So we are targeting that audience with this post. Our message is short with a catchy CTA and we also include hashtags.

GOOGLE MY BUSINESS PAGE

On top of your social media posting with Hootsuite, another free and useful tool is your Google My Business page. Have you ever searched for a business on Google? If you have, and the business has been verified by Google, it will pop up in your search results. You can have this option for your business too, and then you can post to your business page at the same time every week as you are posting to your Hootsuite account. This will boost your online presence. Go to www.google.com.au/business/sign-up to create your account. You will have to wait for a code to be mailed to you, then you log into your account, add your code, and forever more you can log into your Google My Business page and add posts, offers and also contact and other details about your business.

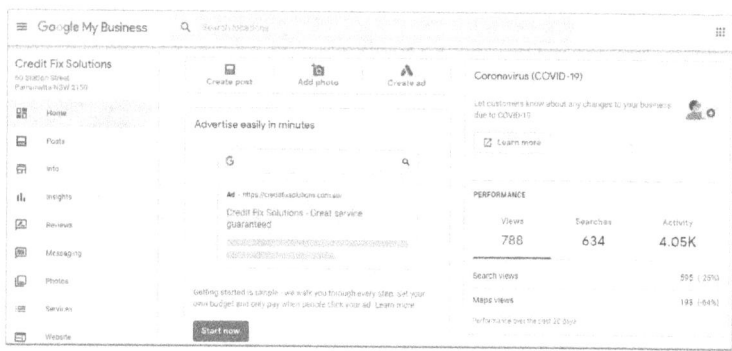

The above is a screenshot of one of our Google My Business pages. You can see that it is easy to click on Create Post, then you add your image and message, in the same way as you add your posts on Hootsuite. Make sure to check your messaging and tweak when necessary so that it speaks to the general public as a whole. Don't forget to include your contact number and your website, so that anyone interested in your product or service can easily get hold of you.

So now we've covered social media posting! You've learned how you can get this done on just one day a week, and you will be in front of your network audiences as much as you like.

# CHAPTER 6
GETTING VISIBLE

- **WEBSITES**
- **LANDING PAGES**
- **BLOGGING**
- **VIDEOS**
- **EMAILS**

IN THIS CHAPTER we will look at key points to do with your website, landing pages, blogging, videos and emails. While this is not a step-by-step, 'how to' guide to setting up your website or landing pages, it does contain great tips to get you started.

CREATING YOUR WEBSITE

You don't need a whiz-bang ten-page website with contact forms, etc. to be able to start earning money. That sort of project can cost you a lot of money, and we are trying to get you started with zero cash right now.

As I explained early in the book, you can use networking and social media – especially LinkedIn – to create connections and start talking to people or other businesses about how your services can add value to their business. I didn't have a website at all when I started. I think I created a basic website about six months into my business, when I had established a small but solid referrer network. It cost me around $1,500 to set up, comprised four pages and I created it using WordPress so I could go in and edit the pages myself. I sat with a local website developer whom I had met at a networking event in Parramatta, he showed me how to add data and photos to posts on my website and I went from there.

Hopefully, having reached this stage of the book, you have been networking for a couple of months at least and have some money to put towards a basic website. If not, go and grow your network a bit more and then come back to your website.

If you do have some cash at this point to throw at a basic website, here are my top tips for creating a website:

- Get some quotes from local website developers. Look for someone who will sit down with you and show you how to use your WordPress website.

- Type up the copy for your web pages in a Word document. Look for and save images that you want to use on the pages. Make sure you are using 'free for commercial use' images. This will save you money as the developer won't have to put these together for you.

- Start with a home page, 'About Us'; blog page and 'Contact Us'.

- Ask your developer to set up the blog page so that you can add new posts as often as you like.

- Make sure your website is 'mobile friendly' (your developer will know what this involves).

- Make sure your 'Contact Us' page sends the information someone completes to your email address.

- Have a 'Thank You' pop up if a visitor opts in to be added to your database or submits a contact form.

WRITING BLOGS AND ARTICLES

When I started my website, I wrote blogs in batches of ten and posted one of them on my blog page every week. After around 12 months, the organic ranking of my site had grown considerably. I was hitting page one on Google for search terms, and the only expense was my time in writing the articles and publishing them.

Now, it might seem hard to you right now to think about titles for your blogs and writing them, so here's your hack. Once a month, put a day aside for blog writing. Add this to your calendar now, as a task or event, (I do this in my Google calendar). I allocate the last Saturday of every month for writing my blogs. The second part of this hack is getting your blog titles together. *What are you going to write about?* Coming up with blog titles every month sounds daunting, but you have some help at hand. Search 'Blog Topic Headline Generator' and you will come across websites that will generate blog topic headlines for you once you put your keywords in.

For example, I went into www.impactbnd.com/blog-title-generator/blogabout and typed in 'Home Cooked Meal Delivery Service' and the site started generating blog titles for me. I clicked the 'heart' button every time I liked a headline and it created a list for me.

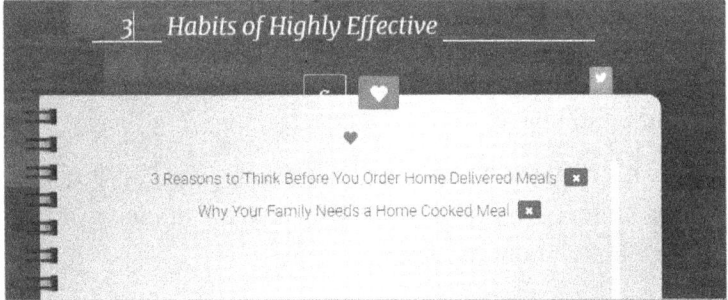

Within two minutes, I'd already created two new blog titles relating to a home-cooked meal delivery service! How easy is that? Go and search for some blog title generator websites, find one you like, and add it in your calendar reminder to write your four blogs each month.

Tips for writing blogs

We have an SEO (search engine optimiser) tool on our website that helps me gauge the SEO effectiveness of my blogs – in other words how great a reach I am getting when I post them. But you don't need to worry about that for now. Just focus on getting posts onto your website, every week, for at least a few months, to help your organic ranking.

Now for some blog-writing tips:

- Use the keyword from your blog title in your first paragraph.
- Make your sentences short, fewer than 25 words.
- Use subheadings every few paragraphs to break up the text.
- Use your keyword in your title a few times throughout your blog.
- Add in an image.
- Make sure you alt text your image with your key word (the alt text is a brief label for the image – hidden from view but it shows up for SEO).
- Write around 300 words per blog.
- Add 'calls to action' (CTAs) in the middle and at the end of your blog.

- Share your blog on your LinkedIn page with a link to your website. (Remember, the more clicks you get to your website, the better your ranking will become!)

Feel free to ask your web designer how to post a blog, add an image and add alt text to the image. I'm sure he or she will be happy to go through this with you.

Now you're ready to get your website up and running and create some articles.

CONTACT US

For your 'Contact Us' page, you want a simple form to request the visitor's first name, last name, email address and mobile number. Ask your developer to set it up to have the completed forms sent to your email. This makes it easy for you to contact any lead that goes to your website from your emails. Later, you can have these forms trigger into your CRM system and create email and SMS responses, but you don't need that for now.

ABOUT US

Don't use stock images on your About Us page. Use photos of yourself, your products or services and/or your office. You want people to connect with you, and so you need your site to be as genuine as possible. In fact, always try to use real images on your website. You can include reviews from customers on your About Us page. We will talk about reviews in the final chapter.

LANDING PAGES

A landing page is basically a one-page website. It can be a lot cheaper and easier to create a landing page when you're starting your business and it's fine to do this. Your landing page needs to talk about your product or service and have a CTA to encourage people to get in touch with you. Developers on Fiverr.com will create and host a landing page for you at minimal cost. Of course, you won't be able to post on there to increase your organic ranking, but at least you'll have an online presence and you can include the URL of your landing page on your business card. Having an online presence creates trust with potential customers or referral partners. If you're not ready to get a simple website made yet, just get a one-page landing page up and hosted, so that people can trust that you are a real business. However small it may be, get onto that right now. Your landing page is going to be a simple call to action page and should be mobile-friendly like a website.

EXAMPLE LANDING PAGE (you're welcome)

Image across the top from Shutterstock:

Web address: www.examplelandingpage.com.au

Slug: Get your free online credit report

Meta description: Improve your credit score today and get a free credit report and free consultation. Get the loan you need!! PH: 1300 43 65 69

Keywords: 'free credit report' 'improve my credit score' 'fix my credit score' 'credit repair' 'credit repair Australia' 'how much does credit repair cost' 'credit repair' 'credit repair Australia' 'credit wash' 'fix my credit' 'free credit repair' 'best credit repair service' 'credit card consolidation' 'real credit repair' 'free online credit report' 'self-credit repair' 'does credit repair work' 'how to fix credit score'

Alt text for images: web address

***Title:* FREE ONLINE CREDIT REPORT**

***Heading 1:* As the #1 trusted authority in credit repair Australia-wide, Credit Fix Solutions offers free online credit reports, and affordable, no-win no-fee credit repair services so you don't pay anything unless we show you a cleared report with an improved credit score.**

Heading 2: Free online credit reports can be available to you within 10 days!

Heading 3: Credit Fix Solutions can help you get a copy of your credit report for FREE and offers a free consultation on the report so you can work out how much credit repair will cost you.

Paragraph: Are your interest rates too high? Do you feel that you were unfairly defaulted by a credit provider? If you answered yes, then you should either give us a call or contact us today *[link to the Contact Us page]* so we can help improve your credit report and look at getting you better interest rates. But how much does credit repair cost?

Paragraph: Get your free online credit report [link to more information about this]. We offer no-win no-fee credit repair Australia-wide. That means we do the work first and then, if we are successful, you pay our fee, which is a set fee, and doesn't change, regardless of how many hours we have to put into fixing your credit.

Paragraph: Improve your credit score. We can remove unjust defaults (also known as overdue listings) and court action (also known as default judgments) from your credit report.

In 99 per cent of cases, we DO NOT CHARGE anything upfront AND we have payment plans available for successful removals. Get your free credit report today and fix your credit fast.

Paragraph: Whatever your situation, we promise to offer you the fairest service in the country and you will be told upfront how much does credit repair will cost you! Get your free consultation *[link to further information]* on your credit score today!

Call to action: Contact smart form requesting first name/last name/email/mobile

(Smart form data to link to email address: info@creditfixsolutions.com.au, subject: Lead from insert web address title)

Paragraph: Credit repair in Australia has a bit of a bad name, but here at Credit Fix Solutions we are slowly changing that. Our CEO Victoria Coster is our resident Credit Repair Specialist, and you will be dealing directly with her in regard to your credit repair.

Get a free consultation *[link]* with our CEO today.

Paragraph: When you apply for our services or contact us [link] you will also receive a free consultation with Victoria, which is a highly valuable consultation, considering Victoria has helped thousands of Australians fix their credit.

Paragraph: Don't be put off by credit repair companies that charge upfront. We will NOT charge you any upfront fees so you can be confident when asking us how much credit repair will cost.

Call to action: **Speak to our National Helpline today on 1300 43 65 69 (plus include a contact smart form requesting first name/last name/email/mobile/ my story).**

Bottom banner (Credit Fix Solutions Banner again)

Get your web developer to host your landing page or website for you. We use www.netregistry.com.au/web-hosting to host our website and landing pages. Once they've sorted out the hosting, then you will have access to your WordPress site! Congratulations on creating your website or landing page!

VIDEO CONTENT

Now, let's get onto video content. 'Video, video, video' is basically your mantra from here. Creating video content for your social media posting and emails is a great way for you to connect with people and other businesses.

Start by creating a YouTube channel under your business name. Go to www.support.google.com to get help to create your YouTube channel. Don't forget to add the URL of your landing page or website to your 'About' tab.

Now go to Fiverr.com and get someone to design your YouTube banner (including thumbnails).

CTA: Go and create your YouTube channel and then come back to the book.

Once you've done that, you need to create some video content. Have a look at what your competitors are doing, (*if they're doing anything good!*), and then think about your content. As with your social media posting, you want to be educational. Refer back to your social media posts and grab some that you can easily turn into a 60-second 'Top tip' or 'Did you know?' video.

Don't start the video with 'Hi, I'm John Smith from Meals to You'. You only have a few seconds to grab someone's attention, and you'll lose them if you start the video like that. Go straight into your content.

For example, 'Did you know, most meals that are delivered don't contain enough nutritional value? Check out our website for meals that will deliver the nutritional value you and your loved ones need at (say website). I'm John from Meals to You and you can contact me on (say number) if you have a query about our meal delivery service.'

Also, make sure you create a 'Welcome video' for your channel, to tell people what you do, what problems you can solve and the three biggest benefits they are going to receive as a subscriber. Ask them to subscribe to your channel at the end of the video.

Keep your videos short – 60 seconds is good – any longer and people won't watch.

Don't worry about video equipment or microphones at this stage. You can simply start recording on your phone and upload the videos (you may need to compress them first) to your YouTube Channel. Give your video a title and add your script to the YouTube post under the video before posting.

Don't worry about all the bells and whistles with YouTube. All you're looking to do right now is to host your videos on YouTube, and then you can share the link across your social media platforms and via email to get in front of existing and potential customers or referral partners.

At the 12-month mark of your business, you will want to do a business course to hone your skills in all areas of business, including YouTube.

Your audience can become weary of seeing the same sort of thing over and over. So don't keep posting videos of yourself all the time. You can create cartoon videos. (We use www.renderforest.com to do this, but go and research video animation platforms. There are loads out there.) If you post a fun, 60-second animated video every few weeks you'll have some variety in your posting, whether it's on YouTube, social media or via email.

As with social media posting and blog writing, set a day aside on a regular basis when you create a few videos and upload them to YouTube. Give yourself a reminder once a week, or maybe you'll post every day, depending on how often you want to post. In all areas of content marketing, you just need to be consistent with creating content. Then posting becomes easy to manage.

EMAILS

When you email your database, you need to be informative and to the point. Please don't write long-winded emails! And *don't spam* your database. People will unsubscribe very quickly if you do. You can use your video content to send an email to people once a week. This shows you being helpful, and informative, and they won't mind getting your emails. Make sure you have a catchy subject line for your email. For example, 'NEW! Free eBook on DIY flower arranging attached'. The words 'Free', 'Did you know', 'Top tip(s)' do very well. Don't be salesy in your emails, remember you always want to be educational and ask yourself how you can add value to the person or a person's business by contacting them. If you're using Mailchimp, you can send your videos or other content to your contacts in bulk. Also, don't forget that you can post videos to your Google My Business page too!

So, you've completed chapter 6. What's your reward? Don't forget to keep rewarding yourself. Now I've finished writing this chapter I'm going to reward myself by taking the rest of the day off!

CHAPTER 7
NETWORK AND CONNECT

- **WEBINARS**
- **PUBLIC SPEAKING**
- **WORKSHOPS**
- **TRAVEL**

WE HAVE GONE THROUGH networking and the importance of creating your social media profiles to connect to relevant people and businesses. Hopefully by now you have quite a few connections, you'll have already had some successful meetings and you're busy scheduling your online content via Hootsuite or other social media posting platforms. This chapter will build on your networking skills and help you connect with relevant customers or referral partners via webinars, workshops, public speaking and travel.

As workshops and travel will cost you money, I suggest you start with webinars and public speaking.

WEBINARS

To run a successful webinar, you will need the following:

1. Content and images
2. Microsoft PowerPoint software
3. An audience to share your webinar with
4. A platform to host your webinar.

To date, you should already have connected with people via networking and your online social media channels, and you should have created an Excel spreadsheet with the contact details of all these people. (Remember to maintain two lists: a client spreadsheet and referrer spreadsheet.)

So why not send everyone an email inviting them to attend an informative one-hour webinar?

We just need to cover points 1 and 2 above – organise our content and images and create a PowerPoint presentation.

To cover point 2, seek advice from someone in your network if you're unsure how to create a presentation in PowerPoint. By now you should have connected with several other awesome business owners in your area. I'm sure for the cost of a coffee or a light meal, they would be happy to sit with you for half an hour or an hour to teach you the basics of PowerPoint. Or there are always training videos on YouTube as well.

For point 1, put a day aside to draft your presentation and remember to make it educational and informative. What can you teach people in a 50-minute presentation (leaving you 10 minutes for questions)? Of course, you can do a shorter webinar – a 30-minute webinar is OK too – again with time for questions afterwards.

My top tip, when you are planning your webinar, is to end your presentation with an offer. For example: 'I've put a great eBook together', or 'I've put a great video together, which I would be happy to share with you on [topic]. Just shoot me an email after the webinar and I'll send your copy out.'

This will encourage people to reach out to you.

Basically, you want to create a CTA in the same way as you do in your social media posts.

Once you've created your content and your PowerPoint presentation, then you must send out an email invitation to your existing connections to see if they would like to attend. We use Zoom to create meetings; it's easy to set up, and free for a basic account (www.zoom.us), which covers point 4.

Think about promoting your upcoming event in your social media posts. Maybe you can schedule some content to go out to LinkedIn and Facebook three weeks, then two weeks, then a week before the webinar goes live. You may attract new leads or referral partners in this way. Remember to make sure that you email everyone after they have attended the webinar and thank them for their time. This is another opportunity to give them your contact details should they wish to reach out for more information about your product or service.

PUBLIC SPEAKING

I have never enjoyed public speaking. Some people find it natural and exciting, while others suffer mild to severe anxiety when speaking. I have severe anxiety about public speaking – to the point where my doctor had to prescribe beta-blockers to try to stop the adrenalin from causing me so much stress. Over the years it has never got easier. I don't sleep well for a few days before public speaking, and the morning of the event I feel physically sick. I push through it, and force myself to speak, but only when necessary.

You may find that you enjoy public speaking. Try starting with small groups. If you've already started your networking and joined local business groups, then you will probably be standing up and doing presentations regularly by now anyway, or at least attending events and giving your 60-second pitch.

Funnily enough I love being in front of a camera, and I don't mind doing webinars. Just don't ask me to stand in front of 100 people.

The good thing about public speaking, if you can do it, is that it doesn't cost you anything to get in front of multiple people at a time. Sure, coffee catch-ups and one-on-one meetings are great but, in a week, you might only be able to fit in 12 coffee meetings. When you're speaking in front of a group, you can have 20-plus people in the room at any one time. If you like the idea of public speaking, keep getting involved with local business groups, and your local Chamber of Commerce, or associations and groups connected to your industry, and offer to speak when the chance arises. If all goes well, people will ask you back to speak.

If, like me, you do not love public speaking, seek out groups in your area that can assist with public speaking training if you need it. Or hopefully, later on when you can hire someone, you'll be as lucky as me and hire amazing staff to do the talking for you!

WORKSHOPS

Running an educational workshop for existing or potential referrers and clients takes time, planning and money. In 2018, I decided that we would travel across Australia educating finance professionals on credit reporting, and how they could improve their marketing skills.

The whole thing cost me around $40,000. We organised workshops in New South Wales, Queensland, Victoria and Western Australia. The workshops were two hours long and I brought along a marketing expert for added value for the attendees.

Of course, if you have a small, local business, then maybe every couple of months you could run a less expensive workshop in your area. There might be a boardroom that someone will let you borrow to save you on venue costs. You might find a local baker who will provide some cakes in return for promoting their business. There are ways to make workshops cheaper.

We now have business development managers in each state, and every two months they run a one-and-a-half-hour workshop in their closest major city. They use coffee shops or other cheap venues, and we only provide tea and coffee with a light snack. This keeps costs down. We encourage our attendees to bring someone along who hasn't used our services before, and who might benefit from knowing what we do. We market the events on our social media channels as well as via email to our database.

Another way to save on costs is to invite a guest speaker along. You can promote the event on their behalf and ask them to contribute half the costs of the event. I attended a workshop a few weeks ago. There were seven presenters speaking over approximately one-and-a-half hours. We each had around 10 minutes to present, we only paid $50 each, and all 20 attendees got a hot cooked breakfast!

For now, you may not have the money for workshops, but keep them in mind for later. They are a lovely way for you to reconnect with your existing referrers or clients or meet new ones. Again, as with public speaking, you're getting everyone in one room in one day, rather than seeing people on a one-on-one basis which takes up *a lot* more time.

Workshop event planning example

Six weeks before your workshop

- *Set a date and time for your workshop.* Mondays and Fridays don't work as well as the mid-weekdays. Consider people doing school runs, etc., and plan for a mid-morning or lunchtime event.

- *Who are you going to invite?* You can invite your existing database, put out social media posts on Facebook or LinkedIn, and invite people you meet at events over the weeks leading up to your event.

- *Create an invitation.* You can design an electronic invitation and/or print flyers for the event.

- *Research venues.* Choose somewhere where parking or public transport is within easy reach.

Four weeks before the workshop

- *Send out your first email blast to invite people.* Let them know the date and time and that the venue is to be confirmed (but give the suburb as the location).

- *Create a spreadsheet of attendees, then add your list of attendees to the event invite via your calendar.* We create a Google calendar invite and then send the invite that way.

- *Check your numbers.* How many do you have interested in coming? Now you have an idea of numbers, you can go back to your list of potential venues and get quotes from them to host the event.

- *Keep talking about the event.* Continue to mention the event to any new contacts at meetings or networking events.

Three weeks before the workshop

- Send out another email blast to your database.
- Confirm the venue and book.
- Check your attendee spreadsheet.
- Email your attendee list to let them know the event address, parking details, etc.
- Mention the event to any new contacts at meetings or networking events. Get their business card or contact details and follow them up.

Two weeks before the workshop

- Send another email to your database, letting them know that limited seats are now available.
- Check with the venue that everything is OK.
- Email the attendee list. Let them know how excited you are to be hosting them at your event.
- Mention the event to any new contacts at meetings or networking events.

One week before the workshop

- Confirm the venue's address and parking, etc., with your attendees via email.
- Do a final check with the venue.

One day before the workshop

- Visit the venue. Check the space and meet the staff who will be helping you host the event.

- *Organise yourself for the event.* Print out any hand-outs. Maybe you have some merchandise to give away? Pack it up ready to take. Remember to take a pen. Make sure your presentation is ready, and check that any speakers you've invited along are prepared and organised.
- *Send an email to attendees.* Remind them about the event the next day and tell them you look forward to seeing them there.
- *Print an attendee list.* You will need this to tick off attendees when they arrive.
- *Do you need name badges?* You can get labels and write names down, or if you can use a printer and label paper, you can print your labels at home.
- *Now you're good to go.* Enjoy your event!

Don't forget to send a thank you email to the attendees the day after the event at the latest. Add a CTA to the end of your email. What goods or services do you offer that they could get in touch with you about?

TRAVEL

Travelling for business is not as cool as I thought it would be! In my twenties, when I started working in offices, I would see the top salespeople or directors flying off interstate for work. I used to get so jealous and wished I could be higher up on the ladder so I could 'jet-set' across Australia too.

As they say, be careful what you wish for! In 2017, I started travelling interstate to events where I could meet more finance professionals to extend my referrer network. From

2018 through to 2020, I spent about half my life on planes, in Ubers and in hotels. Travel took up around half my year. Almost every week, I had to fly interstate and stay for a couple of nights and then fly back to Sydney. Little did I know the level of logistics needed for travelling interstate on business. This is what you need to prepare yourself for, should the need to travel arise:

- Plan your visit at least one month in advance.
- Book flights.
- Book a babysitter/organise family to help with childcare.
- Two weeks out, confirm your visit, the attendees and the event location.
- A week out, double-check everyone is still coming to meetings or the event is still going ahead.
- The day before, plan meetings, organise kids, organise fridge and clean house and school uniforms for the next day. Prepare the kids for the travel plans for the week.

And just when you think you've done it all, then you need to get to the airport, check in, fly interstate, book into your hotel, organise for the event or meetings, catch up on emails over a dodgy hotel meal and try to sleep in a bed that you're not used to – all while feeling guilty about leaving your hubby or family to look after the kids at home.

When you get home, you're exhausted, but you still have to work, and then get back to cleaning the house, cooking, etc. Need I say more?

Travelling for work is far from what I thought it would be. It's tiring and requires a lot of energy. However, if you're running a small business from home, and you target locally, then you shouldn't ever have to travel for business. If you're like me, though, and your local business becomes successful and you dream of serving people interstate, I wish you all the best with your travels and Godspeed!

I hope this chapter has given you more insight into what you can do to connect with people more and more as you grow your business. Don't worry, some parts of travel are fun… you might get a free upgrade to business class with the points you collect and, sometimes, you can score a beautiful hotel room along with some yummy food options!

CHAPTER 8
THE SUPER-DRY BUT NECESSARY

- **LEGAL STRUCTURES**
- **ACCOUNTING**

YOU HAVE A FEW OPTIONS for the type of structure you use for your business, and each one will affect such things as your level of control, regulatory obligations, the amount of tax you pay, health and safety in the workplace, compliance responsibilities, and the level of personal liability that you will incur.

First, I'm going to talk about business structures in Australia, but the bookkeeping section of this chapter applies to anyone in any developed country. At the end of the chapter, I will talk about business structures in other countries as well.

AUSTRALIAN BUSINESS STRUCTURES

Sole trader

This is where you register yourself personally as the sole owner of a business. That means you are responsible for all legal aspects of the business, but you can hire people to work for you. It's the cheapest and simplest structure to operate in, but it does expose you to unlimited personal liability.

Company

A company is a commercial entity/business that has a separate legal existence to its shareholders. It's great for limiting the tax you pay and can provide directors with asset protection.

Partnership

A partnership is a business where more than one person and/or entities run a business together, but not as a company. It's been said that 'a partnership is a ship that never sails'. I would never suggest you form a partnership. I've seen many people burnt by their business partners. It's very risky as each partner has unlimited liability for what the other partner does.

Trust

A trust is an entity that is in possession of income, property, or any other assets, for the benefit of a third party. Trusts are really good for asset protection and provide very flexible income distribution options that may allow you to minimise your taxes.

GETTING AN ABN

If you want to test out your business for a few months, then I would suggest just getting an Australian Business Number (ABN), along with a business name, and being a sole trader for those first few months. You can change your structure when things start to take off.

You must have an ABN in Australia to run a business. Your ABN is a unique 11-digit number that identifies your business or organisation to the government and community. Once you have your ABN, you will be able to register your business name, claim taxes such as Goods and Services Tax (GST), and identify your business to other entities for things like sending invoices or ordering goods and services.

You can register your ABN and business name separately, but it's easier to do both at the same time and here's the link: www.register.business.gov.au.

Note that the registration for your ABN is free. The cost of registering your business name with the Australian Securities and Investments Commission (ASIC) is $37 for one year or $87 for three years (as of August 2020).

When you get to the www.register.business.gov.au webpage, click on the 'Get started' link (see below):

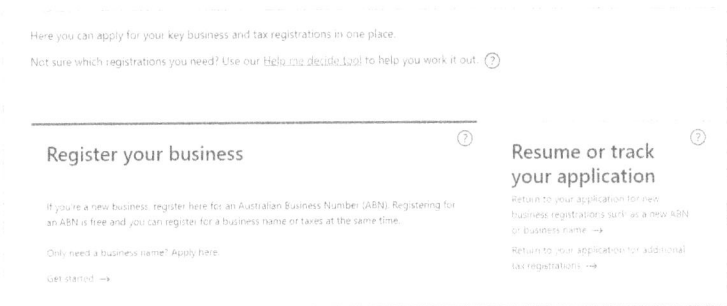

Then, on the following page, select Australian Business Number (ABN) and business name:

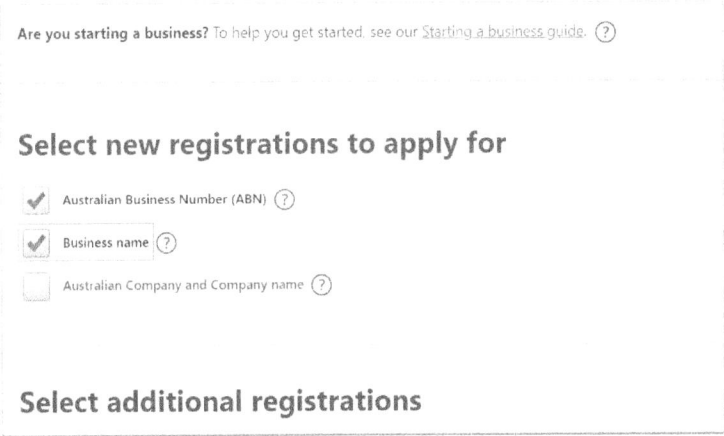

You can register for GST now; the box is just underneath in additional registrations. If you're not sure how much you're going to earn, or you know it's going to be a few months before you earn anything, then don't worry about these boxes for now.

After you've registered your business, you need to open a bank account to keep track of your business income. Your current bank will be happy to assist, although you might want to shop around first to check on bank fees and charges.

Even though a sole trader isn't required to have a separate bank account, it's better to have one. A rule of thumb with income is to save 25 per cent of the money you earn and put that towards tax and funds for business investment.

Once you start earning money, you can engage a local, trusted accountant to assist you with the next steps for your accounts and bookkeeping tasks.

Also, once you have your ABN and business name, you can use these to organise your stationery and marketing material (e.g. letterhead, email signatures and business cards).

Head back to chapter 2 to carry on with your action plan now, or feel free to read the rest of this chapter and then head back to chapter 2.

BASIC ACCOUNTS MANAGEMENT/BOOKKEEPING

When you're starting a business from home, you won't need to sign up for Xero or other complex accounting systems at first. But it is important that you create a solid foundation of bookkeeping that is effective and accurate at tracking expenses.

From the beginning, please keep a copy of all receipts for expenses. If you pay for coffees or light meals at meetings, make sure you record the purpose of the meeting on the receipt, and who you met with. Keeping a meeting in your calendar is also fine if you ever need to prove you had a meeting on the date of a receipt for food or coffee.

You can use a simple Excel spreadsheet to keep track of income and expenses for the first few months, especially if you're not even registered for GST yet.

> To help you get started, I've organised with a business specialist accounting firm called Key Business Accountants to provide you with a spreadsheet and other useful resources that you can download and use for free.
>
> In addition to the spreadsheet, they have agreed to provide all my readers with a free 30-minute consultation with one of their accountants, valued at $150.
>
> To access the spreadsheet and other resources or book in your free consultation, just go to www.business.accountant/zero-to-ceo and use the login code 'StartUp'.

Starting a business from home is a good way to keep your overheads low, and you'll qualify for some unique tax breaks. For example, you can deduct the proportion of your home that is used for your business, as well as internet and mobile phone bills and transportation for business purposes. You can also claim for fuel expenses for work travel.

Keep receipts for everything

I suggest taking photos every day of your business receipts and storing them electronically in a bookkeeping folder on your computer or a free cloud storage facility. Make your bookkeeping a 'must-do' task every day. That way, when you go and see an accountant, it will be a lot easier for you to share these receipts with them.

A few months into the business, once you're earning money, you can go and see a local accountant. They will assist you with any bookkeeping and accounts work as needed. Make sure your accountant understands small business accounting.

You might be able to manage your bookkeeping yourself, and then just use an accountant to organise your BAS and tax returns. An accountant can also help you to:

- Monitor your cashflow
- Look at your profit and loss
- Understand profit and loss projections
- Look at what you are earning and spending
- Keep an eye on your cash position as a whole.

Once a month, try to look at your business as a whole, to understand how your finances are going and get a feel for the bigger picture. Every month have a look at your expenses too. Maybe there is a cheaper supplier you can use, or potentially a supplier could start offering you discounts if you're starting to order more.

We use Xero for our bookkeeping and accounting. I find it a great bookkeeping system. You could use Quickbooks, alternatively, which a few friends of mine recommend. Speak to your accountant about which system will best meet your bookkeeping needs, and work out whether you want to do this yourself or hire a bookkeeper to help you.

Ts & Cs, PRIVACY ACT FORMS AND COLLECTING PERSONAL DATA

If you have a website or you are collecting personal data, you need to have a privacy policy that covers this. On your website, you should have a 'Privacy Policy' page. If you search for 'privacy policy page template' or 'privacy policy generator free template' you will come across sites that offer free privacy policies. You will also need to use this privacy policy in your application form, if you use one for clients. If you have any particular terms and conditions (Ts & Cs), make sure these are also on your website and on any forms you create that clients are signing.

STARTING A BUSINESS IN THE UK OR THE US OR ANYWHERE ELSE ON THE PLANET!

As I'm based in Australia, I've included the steps to register a business from an Australian standpoint. However, all other parts of this book can be applied if you are starting up your business in any developed country. Facebook and LinkedIn strategies in the book can be applied in France, or England or the US. The information about websites can be applied wherever you are and Ontraport and other database systems are available no matter where you live, if you have access to good internet services. Vistaprint and Fiverr are available worldwide, Hootsuite is an online platform you can use anywhere in the world, and networking is networking, no matter where you live.

I've added some information over the next few pages about the legalities of setting up a business in the US and the UK.

I'm sorry I couldn't include every country! But if you're reading this in another country, you can search for information on your government websites on how to register a business name and run a small business. Or you could offer to buy your local small business accountant or financial adviser a coffee or a light meal, and ask for their advice on how you get started.

Maybe there is a local business group that you could join or attend as a guest? Business groups usually allow you to attend at least one networking function for free to test the waters. As a business owner myself, I know that I love to help other people with their businesses and I'm sure there will be a local business owner who would absolutely love to help you get started.

From my recent research, starting a home-based business in the UK or the US as a sole trader, from a legal standpoint, is comparable to starting one in Australia.

Remember, you're *just* starting out, so you don't need a company structure yet. As mentioned, once you start earning money, then you can get legal and financial advice from your local business colleagues with whom you would have already connected. They can advise you on how to organise your legal structure to suit your business. Starting as a sole trader is sufficient until such time as you require other legal structures to run and protect your business.

Starting a business in the UK

If you're in the UK, take a look at this great government webpage on starting as a sole trader: www.gov.uk/set-up-self-employed. Once you've named your business, you don't need to register it, if you operate as a sole trader (it's super-easy!).

However, you must make sure that the business name you choose is not the same as an existing trademark. You can apply for a trademark too at this stage if you wish. You will also have to register with Her Majesty's Revenue and Customs (HMRC) and let them know that you pay tax through self-assessment. You don't need to register for VAT until your turnover is over £85,000 per annum. There are other rules that apply, too; for example, your business name cannot include sensitive words or expressions – how English is that! You can check all the rules via the website link given earlier, which also gives you helpful information on your responsibilities as a sole trader and other pertinent help with setting up a business.

Starting a business in the US

In the US, you have a great government website, www.usa.gov. Once you're on the site, go to the 'Small Business' link and click through to learn how to set up as a sole trader. You will need to search the business name register to make sure that you don't pick a name that someone else already has, then register your business name, investigate trademarking, get a tax ID number and possibly file for appropriate permits, licences and insurances.

><><

Whether you are in Australia, the UK or the US, a sole proprietorship is simple to form and gives you complete control of your business. It's not a separate business entity, so you will be held personally liable for the debts and obligations of the business, but you can still apply for a trade name.

Small business start-ups are low risk, so a sole proprietorship is a perfect vehicle for you to test your business idea before forming more formal business structures.

Wherever you are in the world, I sincerely wish you all the best with setting up from a legal standpoint and encourage you to reach out to your local business groups for help with your legal set-up.

CHAPTER 9
CUSTOMER SERVICE

- **VALUES-BASED SERVICE**
- **CUSTOMER REVIEWS**

GOOD CUSTOMER SERVICE

Every single part of your business is going to mirror your core values, including how well you service your customers. I believe that a big part of my business success has been due to my focus on offering consistently higher customer service than other companies in my industry.

What are your core values?

To work out your core values, write down a list of all the values you can think of. Then narrow the list down to six to eight of the values that you feel stick out from the others. If you can't think of any, think about a few people who you love and look up to. What are the main things you love about them?

I have tried out a free values clarification program, which you can find here: www.lifevaluesinventory.org. You get a 'values profile' at the end of the program. Bear in mind that your values will change as you get older. What you value when you're 20 years old is going to be different to when you're 40, for example.

My core values are:

1. Integrity
2. Equality
3. Accountability.

Integrity translates to offering honest advice to my clients and referral partners when it comes to their credit reports, maintaining my business as a trusted advocacy service for the

Australian community and having a long-term vision for the business.

Equality is a reflection of my core value that all people are equal. I love the saying, 'I am no better than anyone else, and no one else is better than me.' I see my team as my family: we are all on an equal playing field.

Accountability means I make sure that I carry out all my responsibilities as a business owner for customers and referral partners, and I admit to any mistakes that I make and correct them. I am always accountable for the reputation of the business. If any customer has a complaint, I deal with this personally, as this is my responsibility, not my staff's. You're not always going to have happy clients. We're only human, and we make mistakes.

Dealing with negative feedback, complaints or issues – in a positive way – is an important part of your customer service. How do you inspire people when you don't have good news to share?

Below is my five key-point list that I follow and implement to help me inspire people when I don't have good news:

1. Face challenges.
2. Win trust.
3. Be authentic.
4. Earn respect.
5. Stay curious.

There is no point putting your head in the sand when it comes to bad news. However, it is important that we are careful in our approach when communicating bad news. You can use the 'compliment sandwich' method, which means you start with some good news, or some form of encouragement, followed by the bad news or area that isn't working, followed by another compliment.

This method of communicating bad news allows you to win trust with the person involved and shows that you are being authentic and respectful towards them.

If you communicate regularly with people, and actively listen to them, you'll stay curious and be better placed to solve problems before they affect the business.

In addition, make sure that you are building relationships with people, getting to know them outside of work, asking about their families and their personal lives – this establishes trust.

I love listening to people. I am an advocate by trade, so it comes very naturally to me to establish relationships with people, staff and business partners alike. I consider my staff to be my family, and I regularly socialise with staff and with business partners.

A saying that I love is, 'It takes a village to raise a child', and I apply this philosophy to business too – after all, my business is basically one of my children!

Nurturing, loving and respecting people around you will allow you to deliver bad news and make sure that you deal with any issues head-on and as a team.

After-sales customer service is an area in which many businesses fail. They sell a hamper, cut someone's hair, the money is exchanged and then it's just another closed sale.

Businesses often waste the opportunity to make more money from that sale. You should have spreadsheets of clients' details, and it is easy to schedule a task or reminder every month or whenever is appropriate to reach out to them again once you've done business with them.

BUSINESS COURSES

As I mentioned at the start of the book, once you're a few months into your business, and you're starting to earn money, I would suggest looking at improving yourself as a business owner. Think of it as an investment.

We invest our time into our children, into our homes, but what about ourselves?

I thoroughly enjoyed and learnt a lot from Dale Beaumont when I went on his 12-month Business Blueprint Course. If you would like to find out more, here is the link to his free workshop called '52 Ways'. If you're a business owner and are serious about taking your business to the next level, then you simply must attend this FREE business workshop: www.52ways.com/?orid=63315&opid=82.

CUSTOMER REVIEWS

I can't stress the importance of obtaining customer reviews. Whether it's a five-star review on Google or a great email that you get from a happy client or referrer, reviews are extremely valuable for attracting new customers. We all use Google to search for businesses, and it's usually one of the businesses with great reviews that we end up choosing.

Well, here we are at the end! It's been an amazing journey for me to write this book and I sincerely hope it helps you start something awesome! I would love to hear your feedback or any success stories if you would be kind enough to share. My email is victoria@creditfixsolutions.com.au.

Again, I wish all the absolute best for you, your family and your future business adventures.

> *'For I am not ashamed of the gospel, because it is the power of God that brings salvation to everyone who believes: first to the Jew, then to the Gentile.'*
>
> —ROMANS 1:16 (NIV)

www.ingramcontent.com/pod-product-compliance
Lightning Source LLC
Chambersburg PA
CBHW050318010526
44107CB00055B/2292